ORIGINAL
ASTON MARTIN
DB4/5/6

ORIGINAL
ASTON MARTIN
DB4/5/6

Robert Edwards

Photography by Martyn Goddard

Edited by Mark Hughes

Published 1992 by Bay View Books Ltd
13a Bridgeland Street
Bideford, Devon EX39 2QE

Designed by Peter Laws
Typeset by ICON, Exeter

ISBN 1-870979-28-1
Printed in Hong Kong

CONTENTS

Introduction

DB4 from the Third series, belonging to Victor Gauntlett.

There is a little of Mr Toad in many of us, I suspect, at least those of us who admire and possibly covet fine cars. It is not necessarily a difficult thing to admit, after all, and anyone who freely acknowledges his or her obsession to be motor cars has any number of rationalisations behind which to hide. In recent years, they have even assumed the status of investments, although frankly this seems to me to be the biggest rationalisation of all.

The shape of them, the sound of them, even the smell of them, have all played their part in creating an appeal for several generations of enthusiasts. More recently, the price of them has attracted rather more attention than anything else and created several more categories of enthusiast, although at the time of writing this phenomenon has brought with it more than a few tears, I suspect, as yet another perfectly enjoyable activity has been devalued by its metamorphosis into a

'market'. For the moment at least, the appreciation of fine cars is back in the territory of the rest of us, amphibians or not.

For myself, despite the undeniable temptations offered by many marques of motor car, I have always come back to Aston Martins. I have owned or − perhaps more accurately − been the victim of no fewer than five of them, all David Brown models, all risibly expensive to repair and all of them requiring it too. I remain undeterred, my personal rationalisation being, I suppose, that I have met some utterly nice people who share my passion and that I have accumulated a jolly useful quantity of spare parts. This last, of course, represents the reverse of Dr Johnson's famous aphorism concerning second marriages − the triumph of experience over hope. I have been generally a happy Aston Martin owner and would recommend it to anyone, if only because everyone should see, at least once in their lives, what real workmanship and dedication is all about.

This is not meant to be an uncritical hagiography, but many of the subjective comments which have no doubt crept in are, for the most part, the result of my own experience. I am fully aware that other people's encounters will have left them feeling differently: if I give offence, then I apologise in advance. On the other hand, I hope that I am not totally unbalanced where I am subjective, despite the fact that push-starting a DB4 for five days a week, as I was forced to do for a while, is surely enough to unbalance anyone. I therefore throw myself upon the mercy of the executives of any of those companies about whose products I have been less than flattering. After all, it was all a long, long time ago, wasn't it?

I discovered my Aston Martins fairly early in my life, but rather late in theirs. There are, therefore, a host of people to whom I owe a great debt. First, of course, the man who paid for this book — Charles Herridge. Mark Hughes, the editor, has given me priceless encouragement, and I count myself lucky that my first book has the good fortune to be illuminated by such an eminent photographer as Martyn Goddard.

From a technical standpoint, the list is rather longer. I am particularly beholden to Richard Williams, who not only checked the manuscript for technical accuracy, but also allowed us the use of his cars, premises, patience, staff and good name in order to capture on film six of the beautiful machines in this book. Those who already know Richard will not be surprised at this.

John Baldwin and Charlie Prince of Paradise Garage were most helpful, supplying three cars for photography. Special mention also to Paul Dobson, Spares Registrar of the AMOC, not only for assistance during the writing, but also for setting off at short notice, in unpromising weather, to enable his DB4 Convertible to be photographed at Brooklands. The staff at the superb Brooklands Museum, notably ex-Aston Martin man Keith Griggs, were kindness itself in agreeing that so much of our photography could be accomplished at their hallowed site.

Thank you also to the other owners who allowed their cars to be photographed: Victor Gauntlett (DB4), Bob Shapiro (DB4), David Ruddell (DB5) and Brian Tustain (Lagonda Rapide). At Newport Pagnell, Elaine Chapman and Kingsley Riding-Felce kindly made arrangements regarding Victor Gauntlett's car.

Special thanks to Vic Bass, Gerry Pettit, Messrs Pugsley and Lewis, Peter Smith, Ian Moss, Roger Stowers, Ivan and Richard Forshaw, Alan Pointer, Clive Smart, Alan Archer and Richard Zethrin. Lucas Industries, Connolly and ICI provided helpful information, saving me much legwork. There are many others as well. A hint here, a suggestion there, a correction or question, always politely put — these have been invaluable, going a long way toward keeping me on the right track.

Last, and possibly most heartfelt, thanks to Aston Martin Lagonda for making these cars. To own one is to share in something rather special. The text may not always read that way, but this, sincerely, is my conclusion.

Robert Edwards
October 1991

The distinctive nose of the DB4, a third series car.

David Brown Aston Martins Past and Present

A DB4GT. Actually, one of the first ones. Ex-Stirling Moss, this car remains competitive today, a fact hinted at by the livery it wears.

By the time David Brown had completed the purchase of both Aston Martin and Lagonda by early 1948, he had spent over £75,000. On the face of it, he did not get very much for his money. With Aston Martin, he obtained a somewhat rotund prototype, powered by a pushrod four-cylinder engine of rather limited potential but installed in a chassis of great merit, and acquired the services of the designers and engineers who built it, among them Claude Hill. At Lagonda, he became the owner of the Lagonda name, drawings and proto-types, one of which was a twin overhead cam six-cylinder engine designed by the famous Willie Watson. He also became the employer of a host of highly skilled design-ers and engineers, among them Frank Feeley, designer of some of the most beauti-ful of the pre-war Lagonda saloons. In Brown's view, the two firms were comple-mentary to each other.

Both firms had enjoyed an enviable tradi-tion of engineering excellence and both, for reasons not entirely disconnected from this, had had particularly chequered financial his-tories, particularly Aston Martin. Almost a cottage industry, Aston Martin had lurched from crisis to crisis under successive owners who had in common with each other a ded-ication to fine engineering at some expense

to sound business practice. Both firms were based in London, not five miles apart from each other, and both manufactured products aimed at a discerning group of customers. That they had survived so long was remark-able in itself. Several other Home Counties firms, among them Bentley and Invicta, had not made it past the 1930s. To be located so far away from the industrial heartland of Britain was clearly a business risk of some magnitude.

As events transpired, the mating of the Lagonda engine (designed under the super-vision of W.O. Bentley, who had joined Lagonda after the demise of Bentley Motors) with the Aston Martin chassis (designed by Claude Hill) beneath a body styled by Frank Feeley produced a car of startling beauty and performance. There was a price to pay, unfortunately, as the use of the Lagonda engine precluded the further development of the engines which had powered Aston Martin cars up to that point and triggered the departure of designers responsible for them, including Claude Hill.

This car was the DB2, a two seater coupé with fashionable Berlinetta styling, built in alloy on a square tube chassis, and powered by the 2.6-litre LB (Lagonda Bentley) six-cylinder twin-cam engine. The gearbox was, of course, by David Brown. Almost as

soon as the DB2 was introduced in 1950 it was entered in competition events. In 1951, all five of the DB2s entered at Le Mans actually finished, two of them being private entries; although third was the best outright place, the cars were first, second and third in the 3-litre class. As a DB2 had won the Index of Efficiency award the previous year, the car was obviously quite special.

The DB2 and its successors – the DB2/4, DB2/4 MkII and DB MkIII – were produced in relatively large quantities by pre-war Aston standards, some 1725 models of all types being made. The full resources of the David Brown empire were put to work in their production, but even during the life of the first DB2 variant a successor was being sought. Since the numerical sequence of models meant that the first serious competition car which was built at Aston Martin was to assume the name DB3, the successor was to be called the DB4. The DB2 was a hard act to follow, but, as it transpired, so was the DB4.

There was a DB4 on the drawing board as a project at the works of Aston Martin Lagonda as early as May 1955. This car, DP (Development Project) 114, was mooted to be the production successor to the DB2 series of cars for a period during its development, but by January 1957 it had been supplanted by another project, DP184, which did in fact go ahead to the production stage as the DB4.

At the time of the DP114 project, the contemporary production model was the DB2/4 MkII. This car, which was really a redesigned DB2 with a larger engine and four seats, meant that the DB2 series was in its fifth year of production and was ready for a replacement. DP114 bore a superficial resemblance to it, possibly because Frank Feeley had a hand in the design. It certainly used a version of the DB 2/4 MkII's engine, but the chassis and suspension were radically different. The chassis was of the perimeter frame type, used in an attempt to introduce a level of rigidity rather absent in the existing square tube layout. The front suspension used unequal wishbones (as seen on the post-war Lagonda chassis) and the rear end featured a de Dion tube as on the DB3 sports racer rather than the live axle used on the road cars. The de Dion layout, at this stage of its development at Feltham at least, was not yet ready for volume production and, in fact, the public had to wait for the DBS model before it became a standard Aston Martin feature – although anyone who has driven that much-maligned but truly excellent car, the Lagonda Rapide, will agree that this was a pity.

An early DB4 from the second series. This car, owned by Bob Shapiro, is a nice original example, having covered around 60,000 miles. The first series, of which few survive, is outwardly similar, save for a lack of window frames.

This is a DB4 from the fifth series, notable for an increase in body length, to DB5 proportions, as well as an alteration to the rear lamps, establishing a pattern which was to continue through to the DB5. Note the reflectors now present in the rear bumper, and the combined number plate lamp and boot handle, a Volkswagen Karmann Ghia part.

In a sense, it was the use of the perimeter frame chassis which killed DP114. In October 1955, John Wyer flew to Milan to consult with the engineers at Carrozzeria Touring, a firm which was streets ahead of the competition in producing truly lightweight bodywork. They more or less convinced him that the only way to produce successfully their style of coachwork on the new car was by the use of a steel platform chassis, mainly for reasons of rigidity. Thus, DP114 was shelved as a production model by the spring of 1956. A new chassis was to be designed by Harold Beach, Aston Martin's chief engineer, who worked closely with the Italian company through most of 1956 to produce a platform construction of sufficient rigidity to allow the new type of coachwork to be employed. It transpired that the only feature of DP114 which was to survive in DP184 was the steering rack and front unequal wishbone and coil spring suspension layout.

The car certainly looked new. The combined efforts of Touring's founder and head designer, Felice Anderloni, and Harold Beach produced a shape of immortal elegance, which has often served as a yardstick of style over the years. It is perhaps a good idea to examine the two salient features of the shape and to see how they combine to produce a car which, to be a little fanciful, might well have been designed by a car.

First, there is the proportion between the two key focal points of a sports car – the bonnet length and the wheelbase. In the case of the DB4, the wheelbase is 98in and the bonnet length is 60.5in. Divide the bonnet into the wheelbase and you achieve a ratio of 1.62 times the bonnet length. If the wheelbase and bonnet length are added together, and the wheelbase divided into the total, the same ratio is encountered. This relationship is known to architects as the 'golden section'. It is found extensively in classical architecture and can also be observed in numerical series such as Fibonacci sequences, which are often found in nature. Thus, literally and metaphorically, the car has 'classic' proportions. Its wheelbase, interestingly, is only 1in longer than that of the DB2.

Second, there is an almost total lack of adornment. What there is is functional and, with the possible exception of the bumper overriders, extremely elegant. The latter, by the way, are Ford Zephyr items, which may explain that. The radiator grille is extremely simple, whichever type is considered, and it takes as its inspiration the Feeley-designed grille of the DB3S and DB MkIII, adding a certain continuity to the evolutionary process.

While work was progressing on the design of the chassis and body, the third main element of the new car was taking shape under the direction of Tadek Marek, a gifted engineer who had been hired from Austin. His brief was to design an in-line six-cylinder engine of 3-litres capacity capable of being taken out to 3.75-litres if necessary. Being a cautious man, he decided to engineer the bottom end of the engine as if 3.75-litres were the major specification. The bottom end rather decides the size of the engine – the size and number of main bearings having the major influence on the length of the crankshaft. The result was that the engine was much superior as a 3.7-litre unit than it was as a 3-litre, the sheer size of the bottom end requiring the extra displacement. Despite 3-litres being considered as a starting point at the time, Wyer wrote in October 1959, after a 3-litre DB4GT had failed at the Le Mans race the previous June, that ". . . this 3-litre version of the 3.7-litre engine is not a good conception."

So, 3.7 litres it stayed. The result was a car probably rather faster than had originally been envisaged. The original draft specification for the engine required a power output of only 180bhp. As it turned out, the mildest state of tune for this engine has been 240bhp and it has been taken up to a reliable 350bhp. Like the rest of the car, it is perhaps a little over-engineered.

All the various parts came together in the first prototype in July 1957, 15 months prior to the DB4's official launch. Virtually all the 'shakedown' testing was done on the road, including an intrepid 2000 mile journey to the Alps and back in the prototype after it had covered only 500 miles in one piece.

The engine had also been running in another car in 1957. A left-hand drive DB2/4 MkII, with a particularly unhappy mechanical history, had been honourably bought back from its presumably distressed French owner before being fitted with a pre-production version of Marek's engine, stamped 370/PP 300/1185. The car was fitted with Dunlop disc brakes, but not with the wishbone suspension of either DP114 or DP184. It is a particular convenience that this car still exists, owned and restored by Richard Williams, as it goes some way to account for where so many of the development miles were logged, which is otherwise something of a mystery.

The Aston Martin Owners' Club has

The rear treatment of the DB5 is as for the fifth and final series of DB4, whereas the front has been changed to resemble the DB4GT, a feature which first appeared in the fourth series of DB4, generally on vehicles with the special series or Vantage engine.

*The DB6, last of the
DB4 line, is much
changed in structure,
appearance and purpose,
but not to its detriment.*

identified five major series of DB4 (not counting the GT) and I propose to use this format in this book as it is a convenient framework in which to work, despite the fact that cars keep turning up which seem to be 'transitional' models. In fact, though, the DB4 was only offered in three forms: DB4, DB4 Vantage and DB4 convertible. There was a Vantage GT, created by adding a GT engine to a DB4 Vantage, but not, I think a separate model. Furthermore, it is my contention, firmly held as an ex-owner of both, that the DB5 is really only a 'sixth series' of DB4, reasons for which will, I trust, become clear. The connection blurs somewhat with the DB6 and, of course the GT model is less of a variant, more of a derivative.

Anyone who has closely inspected a dismantled Aston Martin V8 will already have observed that it is clearly an Aston, because it looks like one underneath. Disregarding the de Dion rear end and inboard brakes,

the chassis is clearly derived from Harold Beach's work with Touring. The front suspension, similarly, is easily identifiable as being of the same ancestry. The construction techniques are pure DB6 and the engine even has transferable parts. This last cannot be said to be surprising, for the same man designed both. Many of the lessons learned with the development of the straight-six Marek engine found their way into the V8 and thus into the Virage model of today.

The DB4, then, is the common root of all Aston Martin cars made since it was introduced. It is a truly seminal piece of work. As well as being the first car totally designed under the post-war Aston Martin badge, it can be said to be the first Anglo-Italian car, the first post-war car to have a brand new alloy DOHC six-cylinder engine and one of the first to use disc brakes on all four wheels, as well as coil springs. By the time the last

DB6 MkII was made, in November 1970, some 4000 cars had been made which were DB4s or derived from them. All used the Marek engine, which survived until 1973 in the Aston Martin Vantage, the last six-cylinder model produced – under sad circumstances. This was a warmed-over DBS model produced when the firm fell, regrettably, into the hands of Company Developments Ltd.

In common with so many other cars, Aston Martins became heavier over the years, beset as the firm was with demands for ever more comfort and state of the art gewgaws. As we have seen, Marek's engine was equal to the tasks demanded by this growing corpulence, with the result that there is little to choose between the standard models in terms of statistical performance, with the exception of the DB4GT.

The choice is more one of appearance and driving characteristics, between the first DB4, for example, with its rather uncompromising nature, hard springs and light weight, and the last DB6, with its questionable automatic gearbox (optional), air conditioning and adjustable suspension, not to mention electric windows! It is also, I must add, before DB6 owners replace this book on the shelf and walk away, a much more practical high speed touring car than the DB4. Most people who 'know their Astons', and prefer the DB4 as a conception, would point out that as it is with the XK120, the 3.8 E-type, the DB2, the early Aurelia, the first 'R'-type Continental and the Healey 100, then so it is with the DB4. If the designers 'get it right' at all then they generally do so first time around. The DB4, along with the wonderful cars in whose company I have placed it here, can be enjoyed on more than one level – as objects of purely visual desire as well as fine motor cars.

Convertibles often fail to succeed as stylistic exercises in their own right. This is not the case here.

A later DB4, from the third series, owned by Victor Gauntlett. Again, it is similar to the first/second series, but the rear light cluster is modified, to provide separated round lenses.

The DB4

A DB4. It would seem that they got it right first time. Until the demise of the DB6, all these cars were variations on a theme laid down in 1957.

Another car from a different angle. The main external changes up to the fifth series took place at the extremities of the car – the bonnet, boot and corners. Cars will be found with variations to the patterns in this book, and records of small details are fairly inexact. This car, a late Series 3, has a Series 4/5 bonnet, for example, updated to newer specification as the newer design of DB4 emerged. Such variations are not unusual.

We all have our favourites, of course, and the DB4 is mine. This is a Series 3.

CHASSIS

If a car is to be hand-built, then the major design exercise is the one which produces the chassis. The task facing Harold Beach was to produce a platform structure which would overcome the problems of flexing associated with the DB2 series of cars and their putative successor, DP114. It had already been decided to use the front suspension and steering rack from that car by the time the new car was under consideration, but it had come as something of a surprise when the designers at Touring had insisted upon a platform chassis, anything else being discounted as too flexible. The essence of the idea behind the method of construction used in this type of bodywork was that the body frame and the platform should be one, the former accepting some of the loads previously only borne by the latter. It was a radical departure from UK practice and was to have a profound effect on the future design of cars, outside Italy at least.

The chassis of an Aston Martin is extremely complicated, although not in the way that the Mercedes 300SL or the Maserati Type 61 'birdcage' is complicated. Being entirely designed and engineered from scratch, and, for reasons of time and

They came in two lengths – regular and long. This is a Series 5 DB4, with the same wheelbase as before, but a longer body. A quick glance at the distance between the rear wheel- *arch and the bumper reveals the difference from the side. Strangely, the overall proportions are not spoiled, the key visual ratios of wheelbase and bonnet length being unaltered.*

The massive proportions of a DB chassis can be seen from this example, under restoration at Alan Pointer's establishment, Bodylines. This is a DB5, which we can ascertain not just because Alan told us so, but due to the presence of two filler flaps.

The boot floor. This owner is lucky. The weight of the spare has been known to rip the floor out entirely under load.

The floor section is treated in this herring-bone pattern.

money, put into series production almost exactly as it was designed, with no rationalisation involved, it is, to say the least, somewhat over-engineered, in part at least because it was initially assembled at the Farsley, West Yorkshire, plant of the David Brown Tractor company. This has great merit if you are fortunate enough to have a good one on your car, but conversely, if you do not, then restoring it is a nightmare. Certainly, home restoration of the chassis is almost out of the question, for reasons which will become evident.

There are three major areas of the structure. The first, the floorpan, is made from 18swg (Standard Wire Gauge) sheet steel, which has a pressed herringbone swage in order to add stiffness. Two 6in deep box section sills of 16swg steel are MIG (Metal

Inert Gas) welded to it, this whole unit comprising the centre section of the car.

The second section, which might be called the 'pelvis' of the chassis, is the unit which carries the rear suspension pickup points, the rear seats, the tank and the location for the Watt linkage. This is fabricated from inner sections of 16swg steel and outer ones of 18swg. It is this unit which generally suffers the worst from corrosion. The rear axle radius arms are located in 1/8in wall tubes, at 90 degrees to the length of the car and reinforced behind the rear seat support by 16swg bracing. The box section for the Watt linkage, aft of these tubes, is of 18swg steel with internal bracing of 16swg. It should be said at this point that no two chassis are exactly the same, being built by different teams, but everyone agrees on at

least one thing. These structures rot from the inside out, despite the inside faces of the steel being painted, or at least smeared, with zinc paint when new. The rear or second section is probably the most vulnerable, being the most exposed, the most complicated and heavily laden. The boot floor is not load bearing, which is fortunate, as it can rot badly. It sits between, and extends back from, the rear wheel arches, both being made from 18swg steel.

At the upper and lower radius arm mounting tubes will be seen, on an original car, a rounded triangular plate. It is simply spot welded onto the box section behind and serves more as a distance piece than a reinforcement. Many restorers identify this plate as a liability and do not reproduce it, preferring to fabricate the section from one

Full frontal. Note the massive engine cradle and the fabricated bonnet aperture, also the pressed swages in the interior panelling.

piece of slightly thicker steel. This is a matter of choice, of course, but if the plate is not present, it suggests that the chassis has received attention, probably major, possibly skilled. Find out more, for your own sake.

The third area, logically, is at the front, comprising the bulkhead, engine cradle and the front longerons which connect them. The cradle seldom gives trouble unless it has borne the brunt of a crash. It is made from 1/8in steel plate with internal and external bracing of plate as thick as 1/4in. It is the area of the chassis which bears the heaviest single stresses as it carries the engine, front suspension, steering and front brake loads. It is connected to the bulkhead by means of 16swg steel box section longerons, of similar construction to the sills. These join the bulkhead and sills at the bottom of the A-

post and extend two thirds of the way up it. Welded to them are the internal walls of the engine bay, which are of 18swg steel with 28 cooling louvres cut into them. A folded steel frame outlines the bonnet aperture, this being spot welded to the top edge of the engine bay walls.

All the steel sections are MIG welded together on a jig and painted, the internal surfaces with either zinc primer or red oxide, the external surfaces with red oxide only, followed by a second coat of chassis black. The surfaces inside the cabin are left in red oxide. The final attachments to the platform are the jacking points, at the trailing edges of the front wheelarches and the leading edges of the rear ones. The driver's side front jacking point also provides the location for the pedal box assembly. These

points also rot badly, in part due to the fact that no covers are provided for the open ends of the jacking tubes. The platform itself is now complete.

In order to mount the body, a cage of 5/8in diameter 18swg tubes is welded to the platform. These tubes define the main contours of the body, the screen apertures being steel sheet fabrications, like the bonnet space. Where the tubes converge with each other, steel reinforcement is wrapped around them and welded into place. No tubes are needed forward of the main bulkhead, the main point of reference here being the engine bay frame, except to outline the aperture for the radiator grille.

Thus a platform and body frame of modest weight and great rigidity is created. With the engine, transmission and suspen-

A close-up of the Superleggera tubing at the rear of the car and in the roof cavity. Also just visible is the cloth tape used to prevent creaking. It had the unfortunate property, though, of absorbing moisture.

The pedal box. This area of the chassis supports the driver's side jacking point as well as the pedal loads. This component is not usually visible from underneath, being boxed in by 18 gauge steel.

sion installed, the 'running chassis' is extraordinarily stiff, assisted by a very low level of compliance in the mounts for the engine and gearbox and the suspension bushes. The sight of an Aston Martin in this nude form is almost as impressive as when it is fully clothed.

However, these cars do rust. The major difficulty comes from the fact that however brilliant the design, the reliance on contemporary methods of welding and metal closure leaves many points through which water can enter and many box sections where condensation can form. Cynics have noted that tractors seldom have the all-enveloping bodywork which creates these rust-traps, but I have to say that in an accident I would feel safer in an elderly Aston Martin than in certain newer cars. Due to this trait of corroding from the inside out,

however, even sound-looking steel sections often hide serious rust inside them. The general practice now is to replace the probable areas of corrosion as well as the actual ones, this being the only way of gaining access to the interiors of the complicated box sections so that modern rustproofing can be applied.

From experience and a comprehensive survey of owners and restorers, it emerges that the commonest mistake is to pay superficial attention to the chassis, perhaps rewelding the jacking points and pedal box, slapping a few plates over the rear box sections and then spending a fortune on the repainting of the car, followed by reupholstery and so forth. It is better, however, to have a grubby car with a sound chassis than a pretty car with a questionable one. Experience is replete with encounters with cars which have undergone 'MoT quality' welding and which are, frankly, unsafe. Due to the way in which the loads are fed through the complete frame as a function of its design, even a terribly rusty car can feel completely solid. My first DB4 was such a vehicle, much admired and very fast. Only when I had to change a wheel did I realise the full horror of what lay behind the beautifully formed outer skin, as the jack simply sliced upwards through the alloy, taking the pedal box with it as the offside jacking point progressively collapsed.

Having said all that, there are a number of specialists now who will rebuild the chassis properly, but the cost of a comprehensive rebuild is considerable, even approaching the level of a reasonable new car. Some clues about the hours involved are given in the section on restoration. Many of these firms are capable of making a complete new chassis, platform, cage and all, but despite the state of some cars, this is seldom really necessary. Suffice to say that a thorough inspection of the chassis of a car is *the* major priority when looking at a car which may not have received documented, competent attention. The cost of an engine overhaul is, believe me, as nothing compared to a rebuilt chassis frame, not to mention the emotional stress of standing under your car, while it is on a lift, and having it pointed out that your chassis is a lightweight one, by virtue of the fact that so much of it has rotted and fallen off that there is little there on to which any new metal can be welded. That is the point at which you must make the choice between buying a new car, or pressing on with a chassis rebuild, which can easily cost about the same.

FRONT SUSPENSION

W.O. Bentley had specified a wishbone suspension system both front and back for the first post-war Lagonda saloons, which were cars of an engineering quality bordering on the self-indulgent. The trailing link arrangement used for the DB2 series of cars had the twin virtues of simplicity and low cost, but when the DP114 project car was conceived the decision was made to introduce the wishbone system onto an Aston Martin for the first time. As we have seen, the front suspension and steering were the only elements to be used on the new car.

The layout uses unequal transverse wishbones and ball-jointed kingpins, with Armstrong telescopic dampers (type S65/0295) and co-axial coil springs (with a deflection rate of 174lbs/in and 11.7 coils). Kingpin inclination is 5 degrees, castor angle is 1–1¼ degrees and camber angle is ½–1½ degrees. Castor angle is set by the use of up to 16 shims between the outer end of the upper wishbone arm and the bracket into which the kingpin fits. The stub axle bolts through the kingpin and is secured by a ³⁄₄in Nyloc nut and plain washer. Thus the taper roller bearing is held firmly in place with its oil seal between the outer face of the kingpin and the largest radius of the stub axle. The lower wishbone is of one piece but serves two functions. The rear arm is secured, via a split aluminium ball joint, into the chassis longeron, and acts as a brake reaction strut, feeding those loads rearwards under compression into the platform. The front, to which is attached the anti-roll bar, is located via a spindle running through the chassis. The anti-roll bar spindle passes vertically through the forward arm of the lower wishbone and is rubber bushed top and bottom.

Typically, this set-up gives little trouble, provided that it is properly assembled and serviced. The torque loads for setting up the geometry are huge, and it is sensible to check on the presence of the correct castle nuts and split pins. The split aluminium ball joint can jam itself into the chassis through electrolytic corrosion, as the joint is only masked from the elements by a single rubber gaiter, wired on to the lip of the chassis socket. As the socket slowly destroys itself, play develops in the joint, which can be felt and heard under braking.

Experimentally, the set-up was tried in DB3S/10, after the DBR series had arrived. The DBR4 single-seater also used the

Front suspension. The brake reaction strut, complete with its rather inadequate gaiter, is clearly visible. On the other side of the hub, you can see the anti-roll bar. The finish is correct. The dampers are Konis here. The original Armstrongs were blue. Most cars will have Konis fitted.

Rear end. Clearly visible are the check straps, bump stops and damper links. The rounded triangular plate to the right is the mounting point for the trailing arms. Again, the finish is correct.

system, but with the lower wishbone reversed, placing the brake strut under forward tension rather than rearward compression, allowing a rather lighter chassis. All components are finished in a thin coat of gloss black except for the dampers, which were originally blue, but are commonly now red if Koni units are used.

REAR SUSPENSION

A live axle, located on parallel trailing arms, is used, located transversely by means of a Watt linkage. Helical coil springs are again used, but with a deflection rate of 132lbs/in and nine coils, and mounted behind the axle. The dampers, while still originally Armstong, are this time double-acting lever arm types (no. DAS 12 PXP or replacement). The de Dion rear end from DP114

was not used, although one DB4, chassis 170, was fitted with a de Dion layout, more or less as used in the Lagonda Rapide. Bolting the final drive to the platform, particularly such a rigid one as this, apparently produced periods of vibration.

Despite revisionist opinion to the contrary, the live axle layout suits the cars very well. It is simple, reliable and more or less trouble free. The bushes in the radius arms need to be watched, as they support heavy loads. Any ovality in the eye of the arm will cause twisting of the axle. The damper links also need close scrutiny for the same reason.

From chassis 766, Selectaride dampers were offered as an option. They are still of the DAS 12 type, but have four settings, controlled electromagnetically from a dashboard switch which rather resembles a gas cooker control.

This is a Dunlop centre-lock wire wheel, the sort most commonly found on the DB4.

Front brake. It can be seen clearly that the cylinder bore size is cast into the caliper, which makes replacement more straightforward – if you can find the parts.

STEERING

The steering is rack and pinion, made by Aston Martin themselves. It is unassisted, with a column split by a universal joint, which provides for rake adjustment. The rack is bolted, via two mounting plates of rubber sandwiched by two steel plates, into the chassis, which is tapped to accept the four UNF $^5/_{16}$ bolts which locate each plate. Securing straps are fitted over the mounts in order to reduce rack movement should the mounts themselves fail. Although these look home-made, they are in fact original, but curiously are not mentioned in the manual or parts book, which rather suggests that they were an afterthought. It is quite possible that not all cars have them. Track rods are proprietary units, as fitted to several con-

temporary cars, one of which is the Morris Minor. Steering rack gaiters, likewise, are similar to Capri items.

The steering wheel itself is unique to the marque and almost qualifies as a work of art in itself. It is of 16in diameter, using an alloy frame sandwiched between layers of split cane and wood. The layers are all held together with 15 aluminium rivets, the ends of which are rounded and act as finger grips on the reverse of the wheel. There are three spokes, painted matt black, although the edge of the wheel is left in natural aluminium. The rim is varnished and the horn push is blue, with a stylised 'DB' motif. Many cars are found with incorrect wheels, if only because modern reproductions are very expensive. The column is adjustable for reach – basically in or out. Turning circle is 34ft with 2.8 turns lock to lock. Toe in is $^1/_8$in. The rack and the steering column are painted in a thin coat of black paint.

BRAKES

A Dunlop disc brake system is used, front and back. Originally, the prototype DB4 had a disc/drum layout, as on the DB MkIII, but all production cars used discs on all four wheels.

The brakes are hydraulically operated, via a Lockheed vacuum servo. This unit is of the same type as used by Jaguar on the 3.8-litre saloon, and is located on the offside rear of the engine bay. The handbrake is a fly-off type mounted on the driver's side sill. The

This wheel is by Borrani. An alloy rim with steel spokes, it is significantly lighter, but Italian footwear has always been expensive.

master cylinder is mounted on a cast bracket under the driver's footwell, next to the clutch cylinder of type Dunlop VBM4027.

Several changes were made to the braking system in the life of the DB4, before a Girling system was adopted for the DB5 and 6. All Dunlop systems are basically the same, the main changes being to the sizes of the piston and cylinder, to modify the front/rear brake balance. Up to chassis 250, VB1033 calipers were used at the front and VB1046 at the rear. The caliper cylinder bore is 2¹/₈in at the front and 1⁹/₁₆in at the rear.

From chassis 251 to 600, VB1075 were used at the front and VB1103 at the rear. The caliper cylinder bore remained the same at the front, but at the rear it increased to 1³/₄in. The later calipers are simply heavier duty, as are the front discs, the diameter of which increases from 11¹/₂in to 12¹/₈in, although thickness remains at ¹/₂in. Pad size is also increased, so that total swept area increases from 491sq. in to 524sq. in.

From chassis 601 to 1000, VB1188 calipers were used at the front and VB1179 at the rear. From chassis 1001, at which point 15in wheels became standard, VB1198 calipers were used at the front and VB1332 at the rear. If there is any doubt as to the calipers used, the piston bore size is cast into the caliper.

The Lockheed servo and Dunlop master cylinder are the same all the way through, the latter being of ⁷/₈in bore. The handbrake was modified at chassis 601, at which point the pads became detachable from their carri-ers, previously having been riveted to them. Care must be taken in one particular area. The Dunlop system uses a 'positive stop' on the caliper to prevent the pistons from becoming fully extended, so that if discs are skimmed then pad life is reduced, due to the inability of the piston to make up the thickness taken off the disc.

All parts are left in the suppliers' finish. In the case of the calipers, this is silver-grey, with the servo left in cadmium finish. The brake pipes are steel, fixed tight to the chassis by means of steel mounting clips screwed in place.

REAR AXLE

The axle is live, with a hypoid bevel final drive, but usually without a limited-slip differential. The unit is manufactured by Salisbury, type 4HA. The limited-slip differential option is of the Powr-Lok type, utilising the same axle casing. The 'default' ratio for the final drive is 3.54:1, using which the car will deliver 22.6mph per 1000rpm.

It is interesting to note that the gearing available for direct drive top, coupled with various final drive ratios, allows the DB4 a considerable spread of top speed performance. At 6000rpm in direct top, the 4.09 axle affords a maximum of 118mph, the 3.77 gives 127mph, the 3.54 (standard) gives 138mph and the 2.93 produces 165mph. The 3.77 axle, using overdrive top, should allow a shade under 150mph. When determining how fast you want your car to go, perhaps more attention should be paid to which axle ratio you choose rather than how many carburettors you are using.

The swapping of ratios is not particularly complicated, but be advised that two types of differential casing exist, for ratios of 3.54 and higher or 3.77 and lower. The final drive ratio should be stamped on a tag on the differential unit rear cover, visible from under the car. If the unit is fitted with the Powr-Lok limited slip system, another tag should be there too, marked PPL. Of course, despite their differences, complete axle units are interchangeable. Do not neglect to obtain the correct speedometer drive for any other ratio you try.

The capacity of the differential unit is three pints. So far as maintenance is concerned, there is little to do. The axle whine often associated with Salisbury hypoid axles can usually be traced to incorrect backlash adjustment.

WHEELS & TYRES

The commonest fitment to the DB4 is the Dunlop 16in wire wheel painted in silver-grey. Chromium plating was optional, but body-colour wheels were not offered as an option. Three types of spinner are found, all of which use the same hub. First, the usual type is the two-eared spinner, which is unbadged and chromium plated. Second, an

Exhaust side of the engine. Engines prior to number 700 did not have the breathers seen here on the timing chest, but out of sight under the front exhaust manifold. The plug leads should be yellow with a black tracer, rather than this suppressed green type. The cam boxes have been repainted, but the finish looks authentic.

octagonal type was optional in this country, but mandatory in some parts of the continent; a special spanner is used with this type. Third, a triple-eared spinner, also unbadged and chromed, was an option except on the continent.

From chassis 1001, 15in wheels are used, again painted or chromed, with the same variations in spinner types. The hubs are unchanged, whichever wheel is fitted. Many cars with chassis numbers of lower than 1001 will be found to have 15in wheels, due to the preference now for radial tyres and the difficulty of obtaining 16in tubed radials at anything like a reasonable price.

Tyres are of several types, all crossply. The 16in tyre is a Dunlop RS5 or RS7, or an Avon Turbospeed – all will be of 6.00 x 16 size. The 15in tyres are 6.70 x 16, by the same makers. Whitewall tyres were an option for all DB4s but are seldom seen now.

It is possible that a 16in Borrani wheel is fitted, which has an alloy rim with chrome steel spokes. It is an optional extra on the DB4 but standard on the GT model, and is, of course, significantly lighter than the Dunlop product. Both Dunlop and Borrani wheels are available, the latter at quite staggering cost. Tyres of the crossply type are

being remanufactured, but radials remain elusive. It is the firmly held view of at least two of the experts consulted that the cars are happier on crossply tyres anyway, but that also rather depends upon whether the driver is.

ENGINE

The engine began as development project number 186 in 1955. In production form, it is exactly 'square' with a bore and stroke of 92mm, giving a displacement of 3670cc. The block is sand cast in aluminium alloy and has cast iron liners. The crankshaft, made by Laystall, is a Nitrided chrome molybdenum steel forging, carried in seven main bearings of 2¾in diameter. Conventional main bearing caps are used, as opposed to the rather complex system used in the previous LB6 engine, with expanding alloy 'cheeses' holding the crank to the journals. The bearing shells are steel-backed, with bearing surfaces of copper and lead.

Connecting rods are manganese molybdenum steel forgings, with crank bearings of 2¼in diameter. The shells are of the same type as the mains. The rods are weight matched in sets of six to within two drams. Pistons are die-cast aluminium, with two

The inlet side. This is a standard DB4 with twin SUs, which are wearing the correct pancake filters.

compression rings and a twin-segment oil-control ring. The top compression ring is chrome plated.

Oil is pumped by an exterior-mounted chain-driven pump of Aston Martin manufacture, via a full flow oil filter which uses a Purolator MF26 element. Up to engine number 266, a 14 pint sump is fitted. From engine number 267 to 570, a 17 pint sump is used, and from engine 571 onwards, a 21 pint one is used. If an oil cooler is fitted, these capacities are increased by two pints. Oil pressure is high in these engines, or should be. Some adjustment in pressure can be made via the pressure relief valve, but ideally only to lower it. I recently saw a rebuilt engine on a test bed producing 120lb pressure (hot) at 2000rpm. This much is unnecessary, but better to have too much than too little. Ideally, 100lb (hot) at 3000rpm is the target if an oil cooler is fitted, a little less if not. The variance on the clearances at the bearing surfaces is quite large, depending upon temperature, so that the higher the temperature, the greater the clearance, and the lower the pressure at a given oil flow. An oil cooler is as important to increase capacity as to lower temperature; but either way, important it is.

The cylinder head is also an aluminium sand casting. It uses hemispherical combustion chambers with two valves and single plug ignition. The valve diameters are 1.875in inlet, 1.7in exhaust. 'Brimol' iron alloy valve seats are shrunk into the head, the guides being of phosphor bronze. The valve stems are at 80 degrees to each other, the inlet valve having a seat angle of 30 degrees, the exhaust being 45 degrees. The valves are steel, with inverted bucket tappets and double valve springs. Lash is adjusted using tappets of varying crown thickness and by grinding the valve stem.

The camshafts are cold-chilled cast iron, carried in four plain bearings. They are driven by a Reynolds two-stage roller chain with manually adjustable tension. The intake valve opens at 28 degrees BTDC and closes at 68 degrees ABDC; the exhaust opens at 62 degrees BBDC and closes at 22 degrees ATDC. The inlet cam drives the Lucas distributor, which has a black bakelite cap, and copper-cored leads coloured yellow with a black tracer.

The engine finish and appearance is functional rather than flamboyant. The unit is mounted to the chassis by three brackets, two at the front, one at the rear, the latter having two mounts. The mounts are hard discs of rubber, with a steel plate on either

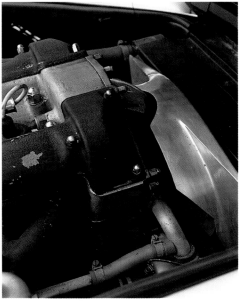

The early engines did not have breathers on the timing chest. No car later than Series 3 should have this configuration.

This is a Special Series engine, with three SUs. There are other differences, also, but they are all internal.

Quite a rare car. A Series 5 with a standard engine. Note the cold air box. Again, the plug leads are incorrect, as is the air intake hose, which should be paper-covered foil.

A good view of a 3.7 GT engine. We know what it is because it has single studs for the cam covers and a dynamo. The finish is correct and is the same for all engines. Of course, only GT engines used these Weber carburettors.

side and a threaded stud running through the middle. The engine bay is painted in a textured matt black paint over red oxide, while the main bulkhead is gloss black. The main castings of the engine are left in natural aluminium, although the camshaft covers are finished in a silver-grey enamel, similar to grey 'Hammerite'. There are 14 head studs, each capped by a chrome plated domed nut. The two nearside studs at opposite ends of the head carry the ignition lead tube, which is also chromed.

From engine number 267, a double engine breather was fitted at the front nearside engine mounting, but moved to the timing cover after engine number 701, where it subsequently remained on all six-cylinder engines. For those owners of a more ostentatious turn of mind, a special 'show' engine was available. None of these is now available for inspection, but the specification included vitreous enamelled exhaust manifold (as opposed to silver grey enamel), black enamelled carburettor bodies, black enamelled servo, polished and plated pipework, and scraped and burnished alloy castings (including the cam covers). The louvred engine bay panels were still covered in textured paint, but this was oversprayed with a thin coat of gloss black – a canine repast indeed. Actually, this was more or less the specification of a motor show exhibit, although cars have been seen at motor shows in standard finish also.

The Tadek Marek engine, then, is not particularly complicated. Certainly there were development problems, chiefly in the area of oil cooling before the sumps were enlarged and coolers fitted, but possibly no worse than those encountered by any other specialist manufacturer. Astonishingly, oil coolers remained optional for most of the model's life, except for those cars fitted with a GT engine. Many will now have been modified, of course, and serious difficulties are only encountered with very early cars, with no oil cooler, at sustained high speeds in excess of 90–100 mph.

The net result is an engine which, in standard tune, produces 240bhp at 5500rpm and torque of 240lb ft at 4250rpm.

Vantage specification simply means a higher state of tune. All the changes are to the cylinder head. The head face is machined to produce a higher compression of 9:1, while valves are enlarged to 2in for inlets and 1.875in for exhaust. Seat angles stay the same. Inner valve springs come from the GT (outers are unaltered), with a deflection rate of 150lb in. Power is raised by 10%, torque by 6%. Carburation is modified also, and is dealt with in that section. Cam timing, please note, is unchanged. Original factory-ordered Vantage engines will have a suffix, 'SS' (for Special Series), stamped on the engine number. As the engine number is on the block and not on the head, it is possible that an after-sale modification, made by the factory, to bring the engine to Vantage specification would not be revealed by this. Likewise, the presence of the 'SS' suffix on the block need not

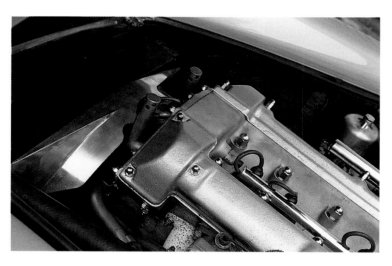

The two-piece fan cowl. Replacements are available but often have to be tailored to fit.

guarantee that the head is a Vantage one. More on this in the section entitled 'Identification & Dating'.

If looked after, the Marek engine is an extremely pleasing piece of machinery, in standard or Vantage tune. It can be extensively modified to produce well over 300bhp with reliability, as has been shown by both the later manifestations of it and the tuning that is carried out today by racers. The unit is often compared with the XK Jaguar engine, but I rather think that this comparison is fruitless, given the fact that the Jaguar unit is designed for higher volume production, has its design roots during the war and has an iron block and a long stroke. Really, it bears a greater resemblance to the LB6 engine as used in the DB2 series of cars, to which it was superior, given its 800cc advantage and simpler design. The Marek engine, running properly, is quite inspiring, given its development time and its budget. It seems to be a generally-held opinion among the cognoscenti that anyone who inserts an XK engine into an Aston Martin is probably also the sort of person who molests infants, cheats at cards and, in all likelihood, wears a vest in bed. It is not for me to share or oppose this view.

COOLING SYSTEM

This is a subject upon which there is much less controversy – it is barely adequate to the task. A crossflow radiator is used, manufactured by Serck, with a capacity of 28 pints, including the separate header tank. The system uses a 7lb/sq in pressure cap. The water pump is an Aston Martin item, externally mounted and driven by the fan belt from the crankshaft pulley. The body is an aluminium casting, mounted in a recess on

the timing case. The impeller is brass. The unit uses a 9lb/sq in seal. Frequently, the impeller can slide on the shaft, reducing water circulation. It is a simple unit, however, and can be reconditioned easily.

From chassis 251, a radiator blind is used, controlled by a chain link from the cabin. A choice of two thermostats was provided – 80 degrees and 68 degrees. From chassis 766, an auxiliary electric fan is fitted, operated either manually or thermostatically.

A Smiths heater/demister is used, type 011-22-9151, with an FHM342 blower, the case being in two parts, either side of the bulkhead. It is mounted centrally, above the transmission tunnel, and its removal and replacement are tasks best left to a friendly octopus. Three demister vents are found on cars up to chassis 600, five thereafter.

Bolted to the water pump is the cooling fan, which has four blades up to chassis 200, eight thereafter, and is painted black. The fan is cowled from chassis 201, in two parts, upper and lower. The cowl is of polished aluminium, but, like the radiator blind, often missing. Reproductions are available. Hoses are black rubber, secured by Jubilee clips. The radiator is finished in matt black, the header tank in gloss black and the steel pipes are cadmium plated.

EXHAUST SYSTEM

Twin cast iron trifurcated manifolds are used, running into twin mild steel 16swg downpipes, which join to two flexible sections under the nearside front footwell. Two straight-through Burgess silencer boxes are placed at the rear, with short chromed tailpipes. An exhaust heat-shield of aluminium and asbestos runs from the front footwell to the rear seat support, but is often missing. It should be bolted flush to the chassis. The exhaust is strapped and clamped to the chassis in a rather Heath Robinson manner. Both mild steel and stainless systems are now available, but vary hugely in quality and price.

CARBURETTORS & FUEL SYSTEM

The fuel pump is an SU type HP item, number AUF 402. It is a double action device which pumps 20 gallons per hour, and is mounted in front of the rear axle on the offside of the car. A frequent problem encountered here is the tendency for one

Single Lucas distributor is driven off the inlet cam. These plug leads are suppressed DB5 types

The brass carburettor dashpot tops are correct. Even DB6s have been seen with them, proving that it's really a matter of what's on the shelf.

half of the pump to fail, leaving the car running adequately well, but unable to run at high speed under load without damaging at least one piston. These pumps are common enough and are fitted to the contemporary Rover models. The location of the pump underneath the car is not quite guaranteed to expose it to loose stones and grit, but almost.

The tank is placed under the rear parcel shelf. It is a single, oblong container, with a filler pipe appearing on the top nearside. Fuel is put in through a combined cap and flap behind the quarterlight on that side. The tank sender unit is accessible via a flap on the rear parcel shelf.

The carburettors are twin SU Horizontal Diaphragm HD8s, with a 2in bore. They are mounted via blocks on the offside of the engine, on water-heated trifurcated cast alloy manifolds, the heating pipes being underneath the manifolds. The float chambers are linked by a loop of neoprene tube. Choke is regulated by a cable running to the dash. The filters are gauze-filled pancake types, made by AC Delco, number EAC11040. These are black, with an AC Delco identifying plate in the centre. The needle recommended at the time was UJ, superseded by UN after engine number 475, but naturally, given the changes in quality of fuel since then, this is a matter for experiment. From engine number 854, the slow running valve screws are not used, the cam arrangement having been modified.

Special Series engines used three SU HD8 carburettors, on bifurcated manifolds, also water-heated. The choke cable mechanism was retained, and from chassis 1001 cars fitted with Vantage engines (not all were) were given a cold air box, which was painted gloss black.

Weber carburettors, standard on the GT model, were never offered as an option on the DB4. Some cars will have had Webers fitted and very good they are too, but this would not have been original. Of course, the factory or an agent might have fitted them afterwards by special request, but records are inexact on this.

TRANSMISSION

It comes as no surprise to find a David Brown unit here. Not being a five-speed device, it naturally has its detractors, but I am not one of them. It is a four-speed manual box with a floor change, type S432. The casing is of ribbed aluminium, as is the bellhousing. Up to chassis 765, a single 10in dry plate clutch is used, but after that a double 9in plate unit is fitted. Both are originally Borg & Beck parts, although the clutch master and slave cylinders are by Girling (numbers 64067608 and 3010224W respectively) whichever clutch is fitted.

Two variants of the S432 box will be found and they may be with or without overdrive. The difference is really only the ratios applied to first, second and reverse, third and top being consistent at 1.25:1 and 1:1 respectively.

Opinion differs, and exceptions will be found, but it would seem that wide ratio boxes were fitted to all cars up to chassis 600, with the following gears: top, 1:1; third, 1.25:1; second, 1.85:1; first, 2.92:1; reverse, 2.52:1.

Close ratio boxes were fitted between chassis 601 and 943, with the following gears: top, 1:1; third, 1.25:1; second, 1.74:1; first, 2.49:1; reverse, 2.42:1.

After chassis 943, the wide ratio became standard once again. The parts book puts

This combined rear lamp unit was fitted to early cars, up to Series 2. It is also found on the Alvis TD21.

Series 3 cars had these separate rear lamps. Note the heavy chrome surrounds and polished back plate.

A close-up of the Hella/VW handle, used here on a DB5.

These rear lamps are the late type, and were carried over to the DB5. They lack the heavy chrome trim, which causes them to be slightly recessed.

BODY & BODY TRIM

When we left the chassis, it had been completed by the addition of a cage of ⁵/₈in steel tubing, MIG welded to the chassis and outlining the general shape of the car. The body sections were pressed into an approximate shape and finally formed on wooden bucks in two main sections: the front, from the screen aperture forward; and the back, from the header rail to the rear of the car. The metal used is a 16swg aluminium/magnesium alloy, of a commercial grade called 'half-hard' – ie, workable.

The edges of the body, forward of the A-post and aft of the B-post, are folded around ³/₁₆in malleable galvanised steel wire. The wire is welded to the relevant ends of the box section sill, the whole structure wrapping around the car to create wire edged wheelarches and front and rear skirts. The engine bay aperture, a steel fabrication, has the alloy clenched around it to create the bonnet space.

Where the alloy meets steel, cotton cloth tape, rather like bias binding, of about 1¼in width, was used to stop any creaking between the surfaces. Unfortunately, as the tape got damp, electrolytic corrosion could set in, damaging the aluminium and giving it the consistency of ripe Stilton. At the front of the car, the grille space is created by riveting the alloy to the tubes, again using tape to prevent creaking. At the screen apertures, front and rear, the alloy is again clenched around the steel fabricated frames. The point of reference, then, is not the steel tube cage; rather, it is the fabricated frames

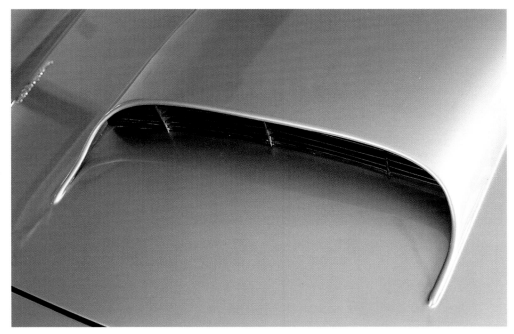

This is the early, large bonnet air intake, containing a small steel grille.

of the main apertures. The tubes merely provide support in the event of the body being stressed. This means that the bodywork is extremely easy to dent, particularly on the front wings and doors, the latter being also steel fabrications, of 18swg. The door apertures have the alloy riveted and screwed into place. The inside faces of the alloy are either painted in red primer or left bare. The steel tubes are painted black, prior to the alloy being fixed in place.

Added to the extremely stiff chassis, therefore, is coachwork of great lightness. Less than 10% of the entire weight of the car is accounted for by the weight of the actual body. In the case of panels such as the bonnet and boot, which are double skinned alloy with no frame, the edges of the metal are glued with epoxy and filed to shape.

No filler is used in the original construction, save for a very thin skim of cellulose stopper applied over the etch primer in the undercoat stage. There will be up to 25 'misted' layers of paint applied to the body, which is not to say that there are that many full coats. Shut lines on bonnet, boot and doors should be around $^3/_{16}$in on bare metal, $^1/_8$in painted. The gap at the bottom of the doors may be a little more.

It should by pointed out that if panels from one car can be accurately fitted to another, then this is a total coincidence, and should not be relied upon as an alternative to having new panels made. A replacement panel for an Aston Martin requires expert fitting, as it is made to fit onto a body which

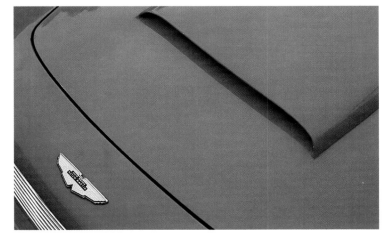

will always be subtly different from car to car. This particularly applies to panels with more than one major curvature, such as a boot lid. More luck may be had with bonnets.

Despite the apparent 'fussiness' of its construction, this complete body/chassis is immensely strong. I had personal evidence of this a little while ago, when a BMW collided with my DB4 at about 15mph, at an oblique angle from the side. The BMW hit the front wheelarch at its forward curvature on the left side of the car. As I got out I had no idea what to expect. In fact, the bonnet shut line was unaltered, and although the car looked dreadful, with great sheets of cellulose paint cracked off it, the damage had been entirely confined to the exact area of impact and cost relatively little to repair.

The later scoop was lower and rather less aggressive. Like the radiator grille, this lasted until the DB6. Unfortunately, when redesigning the bonnet, Aston Martin failed to modify the oil filler cap so that later cars will often be scarred by a pimple caused by the bonnet being slammed when the oil filler has been left open.

Profile of a Series 1/2 car. On this car the bright metal trim is missing from the windscreen surround

Profile of a Series 3/4 car. The slightly protruding rear lamps can be seen.

Profile of a Series 5 car. The extra length can be seen at a glance by comparing the gap between the trailing edge of the rear wheelarch and the front of the rear bumper. This car is 200lbs heavier than the Series 1/2 cars.

The later type bumper, interchangeable with the DB5, which also employed this Hella/VW type of number plate lamp. Reflectors moved from the lamp cluster to the bumper bar. Front bumpers remained similar all the way through.

Some cars will be found with vinyl Webasto sunroofs. Invariably, these were fitted once the car had been made. Due to the fact that there is no natural gap left in the roof for such a fitment, the main transverse section of the tubing has to be removed. This necessitates the strengthening of the roof aperture, as a great deal of rigidity is lost by this process. Ash is generally used, the frames being supplied by Webasto. If present, they should be checked for rot. Replacing a sunroof with a full roof panel is not the nightmare it sounds, and many people feel that the sunroofs are unattractive and noisy.

In terms of the shape of the car, there were a few changes in its production life. The first series of cars, to chassis 250, had rear-hinged bonnets. The first 50 of this series, to chassis 151, had no window surrounds. From chassis 601, the rear lights were altered in the manner already described. From chassis 766, they were altered again. At the same time, the scoop on the bonnet was lowered and the small grille deleted from it. A faired-in front headlamp was offered as an option, generally on Special Series engined cars, from this point.

From chassis 1001, the whole shape of the car changed subtly. The wheelbase stayed the same, but the roofline was raised, having the effect of moving the point at which the roof meets the rear deck rearwards. The whole body is longer on these Series 5 cars, by just under 4in. They can easily be mistaken for DB5 models, for, in effect, this is

The early type of rear bumper fitted up to Series 3 did not have inset reflectors and is very hard to find.

what they are. Oil coolers were standard by now, the aperture being a rounded oblong scoop at the nose, pointing down into the airflow, separately made and attached by pop rivets.

One of the things which makes an Aston Martin attractive is its lack of superfluous ornamentation. The only external items on the car are door handles, bumpers, grille, sidevent flash and very discreet badging. The door handles are bought-in proprietary items, originally manufactured by Wilmot Breeden and are the same as those used on Triumph TR4A and 5 models. They are chromed Mazak die-castings and are being remanufactured – Moss Europe have them under their part number 701560X. Bumpers can be of three types, all of which were (and still are) made by Tuckers of Bristol and all

The early radiator grille, used from Series 1–3.

Triumph also used these door handles on the later TR series.

enamelled winged 'David Brown Aston Martin' badges are found, at the front, forward of the leading edge of the bonnet, and at the rear, on the numberplate light. Finally, two 'Superleggera' badges are fitted at either side of the bonnet, in stylised chrome plated script. They are fastened by three small captive bolts with nuts on the underside of the bonnet panel. These badges acknowledge the method of construction of the body, the technique having been licensed from the Touring company. There is no model badge anywhere on the car, which adds to the confusion when identifying the differences between a late DB4 and an early DB5, for example.

very alike. The first 50 cars had very lightweight steel bumpers with no overriders. From chassis 151, a heavier version of the same bumper was used, with hastily bought-in overriders – an early Ford connection. From chassis 766, the rear bumpers had small circular reflectors recessed into their rear corners, under the tail lamps, the front bumpers being unchanged.

Two types of radiator grille are found, both using the same surround. Up to chassis 765, a simple 'eggbox' design is used, rather similar to the pattern which appeared on the DB MkIII. From chassis 766, the pattern changes to one of eleven horizontal bars, crossed by seven vertical ones.

A simple aluminium pressing runs across the middle of the wing vent on each side of the front wing forward of the A-post. Two

INTERIOR TRIM

The restoration of a car interior is one area where there can be little consensus as to whether an original, tatty interior should be left alone, 'sympathetically restored', or replaced to 'as new' standard. Certainly, a comfortable but slightly worn cabin is wonderful, but to achieve that, a car must have been punctiliously maintained. Unlike the body panels of an Aston, the interiors are rather more easily transferred from car to car, which has given rise to some rather strange colour combinations, the most unfortunate that I have seen being a blue DB5 with a sage green interior from a DB4. Despite the priority of finish being an owner's option, I am sure this could not have been original.

This is the later grille, fitted until the DB6. Note the aperture for the oil cooler.

For some reason, the wing vent is often considered the most distinctive Aston Martin trademark.

The Superleggera acknowledgement to Carrozzeria Touring of Milan.

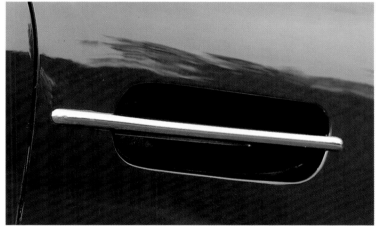

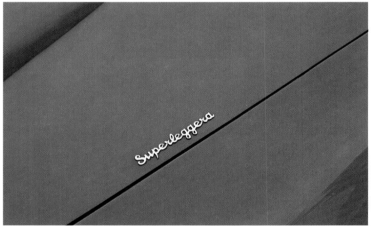

The seats are upholstered in Connolly's 'Vaumol' hide. This treatment, a nitrocellulose dressing applied on a smooth grain, giving a satin finish which wears to a shiny one, is no longer available. Most car upholstery hides now use a water-based resin dressing, which produces a matt but durable finish. An exception to this is Connolly's 'Classic' range, of 13 colours, finished in nitrocellulose, but slightly embossed. If European hides are used in restoration, be warned that many of them have no smell, which, it must be said, is at least a part of the appeal of leather upholstery.

The front seats are made by Reutter, using that patent method of reclining mechanism. They are entirely covered in leather, including the back, which is slightly recessed into the frame. The seat and backrest both have six pleats. The seat is mounted on a runner which allows 7in of fore/aft adjustment. The rear seat is attached to its support by self-tapping screws through steel tabs. Both the cushion and back have 16 pleats, the seat being evenly divided by the transmission tunnel as it is raised to accommodate the differential.

In the rear compartment there are built-in armrests to the rear wheelarches which intrude into the cabin. The arm rests and the arches are also covered in the same hide as the seats. The rear parcel shelf is covered in black vinyl, and has a flap set into the flat surface to give access to the tank sender unit. The shelf is angled up to the rear screen aperture and carries a matt black speaker grille in the centre if a radio is fitted.

Back in the front cabin, the door trims are hide over marine ply, this being unvarnished and secured by self-tappers into the steel doorframe. An elongated armrest/doorpull is built into the door panel half way up, under which there is a full-length map pocket. A ribbed rubber scuff panel, in a bright metal frame, runs from the front of the panel back to the handbrake pivot. The gear lever sits in a leather gaiter protruding from a square let into the carpet over the transmission tunnel.

The tunnel itself is a glass-fibre moulding. The A-post interior is also covered in hide, as is the small box upon which the demister controls are mounted. The sill and B-post are covered in thin sheets of aluminium, secured by self-tappers where they meet the alloy body. The B-post join is covered by a sponge rubber extrusion. On the inboard of the sill, the alloy sheet, which has a

This Series 3 interior is, to say the least, clubby. The seats, by Reutter, are in hide, as are the door trims. Carpets feature extensive rubber scuff mats.

DB4s are a little cramped in the back...but the rear compartment is as sumptuously trimmed as the front.

'wheeled' finish and may be polished or left in natural aluminium, is gripped by a stainless steel trim panel, which also retains a ribbed rubber scuff panel lining the inside face of the sill and tucking down behind the carpet edge.

The carpet itself is wool 'Wilton', and is composed of separate panels, fixed to the floor by poppers and to the leading edge of the rear seat by adhesive. The carpet edges are bound in strips of hide which are shaved from the same hide as the seat covering. The footwells and transmission tunnel both have the ubiquitous ribbed rubber scuff panels built in to them. Under the carpet is a heavy brown felt underlay, secured by the same poppers which locate the carpet.

The doors are capped in black vinyl, retained by a bright metal strip. The locking handle is at the leading edge of the door, pulling back to open, and pushing fully forward to lock. There is no safety catch. Behind and below it is the window lift, in the same position whether it is manual or electric. From chassis 251, the window lift handle was shortened, the gearing on the mechanism being raised. The windscreen pillars are covered in light grey vinyl, with a small graining effect. The headlining material is a cream canvas-textured vinyl, and is the same type as used on the Rover 2000-

Possibly, black is a little more elegant – certainly easier to keep clean. This car has been beautifully retrimmed.

3500 series of saloons; it is available from stockists of Rover Group spares. There are two recesses in the roof, either side of the main transverse members of the steel tube superstructure. These are outlined by two rounded rectangular aluminium extrusions, which are fixed using self-tapping screws. A Lucas 608 alloy dipping mirror is fitted to the roof at the top centre of the screen.

The windows are Triplex safety glass. Up to chassis 250, the rear quarterlight and the doorlights are curved, irrespective of whether the doorlights are framed or not, but they are flat thereafter. The rear screen is of laminated clear glass up to chassis 150, and of toughened Sundym glass thereafter – but they are interchangeable. A heated rear screen is optional for all cars. The quarterlight, which opens about 2in, is hinged via a slot in the rear of the stainless steel quarter pillar and is closed by a hinged chromed clip which actually passes through the light itself. The front screen is either clear laminated or Sundym toughened glass. The sun visors are tinted plastic on a chromed arm, and travel through 90 degrees.

On cars up to chassis 765, an ashtray is flush-fitted on the top of the dash; from chassis 766, this moved to the transmission tunnel. From chassis 251, two semi-circular

DB4 door trim: hide with black vinyl capping.

revolving ashtrays are fitted either side in the rear, set into the rear threequarter trim panel above the wheelarch. If a radio is fitted, it is located in a specially built console, which is fixed to the underside of the dash, just above the gearbox. It contains a mounting slot for the radio and a speaker, covered by a fine mesh grille. The radio is generally a Motorola unit, with an illuminated Aston Martin sign, in red, in the band selector. Aerials are usually fixed at the rear of the front offside wing, if retractable, or on the roof if not.

The boot is covered in black Hardura, but

The vinyl roof lining is a function of the cage above it. Note the chain control for the frequently deleted radiator blind. The sunvisors are of the type found on the Jaguar XK150 fixed-head coupé.

TEX dipping mirror, as fitted to early cars.

The Lucas rear view mirror more commonly found on later cars.

some cars will be found with black carpet – this is not original. On the right is the battery, on the left the jack. Under the floor is the spare wheel well, the tool roll being placed in the wheel itself. The cover is held in place by Dzus fasteners.

Dashboard & Instruments

Three types of instrument layout are seen. On all cars, the dials are enclosed in a binnacle, which bears a passing resemblance to the radiator grille – this style was first used on the DB MkIII. The standard binnacle contains four large instruments. On a RHD car, they start on the left with a combined oil pressure/petrol gauge, the former reading up to 100lb/sq in; after chassis 251, this gauge reads up to 160. Next is the speedometer, which reads to 160mph, and contains the blue main beam lamp and the red ignition light. Next is the tachometer, which is mechanically driven up to chassis 600, electrically driven thereafter – and contains a fuel warning light. Finally, there is a combined ammeter/water temperature gauge, the latter reading from 30-110 degrees.

On this type of binnacle, there is a wash/wipe switch on the left, and below it, a fuel reserve switch. On the right, there is a panel dimmer and below it the headlight/sidelight switch. Two levers are used

A Series 1/2/3 ashtray, set into the dash top.

On Series 4/5 cars the ashtray was moved to the transmission tunnel.

The rolled aluminium sheet on the door shut faces is hard to obtain, and even harder to fit.

DB4GT instrument panel, described later, was generally used, although, like many other aspects of Aston Martin manufacture, it was very much the case that what was on the shelf dictated what went into the car.

IDENTIFICATION, DATING & PRODUCTION FIGURES

The chassis number of the DB4 is stamped on a plate riveted to the right front of the engine sidewall, aft of the radiator. Three pieces of information are given: the model (DB4), the sequential chassis number (starting with 101) and whether the car is left-hand or right-hand drive. So, DB4/946/R.

The actual numbers are also to be found in other places. The main factory identification stamp is, in fact, found on the left-hand side lower chassis near the bottom wishbone mounting point. They are also on a plate behind the A-post, on the chassis, on the top door hinge on the offside, and on the bonnet hinges. If a door trim or the rear seat squab is removed, the number may also be found written in chalk or wax crayon on the reverse. If the car is a convertible, the model type will be suffixed 'C' – DB4C.

If a badly damaged or derelict car comes into your possession, therefore, it should be possible to establish at least its basic number. If you cannot establish whether it is right-

for direction indicators and headlamp flasher, on the right and left of the column respectively, on cars up to chassis 600, but there is only one lever on the right thereafter. To the left of the binnacle, on the centre of the dash, is an electric clock. On the passenger side, above a lockable glove box, a padded grab handle is built into the top of the dash. This layout is similar to that employed on the DB MkIII, the last car in the DB2 series.

From chassis 951, the ammeter was moved to the centre top of the binnacle with the combined oil pressure/fuel gauge being replaced by a combined oil pressure/oil temperature gauge. The ammeter/water temperature gauge was replaced by a combined water temperature and fuel gauge. From chassis 1111, The

An early dash. This Series 2 has three demisters, later cars had five. Note the two stalk controls. From Series 3, a single one was used, on the right. On saloons the dash was painted black.

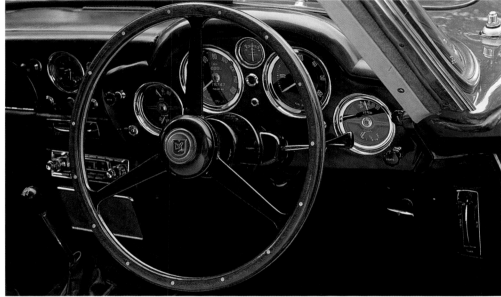

A late dashboard on a Series 5 car. Note the radio console and the single column stalk. The ammeter has moved to the top.

The GT dash, optional on later cars and commonly found on Special Series versions. Combination instruments are replaced by single ones, but the number of functions remains the same.

or left-hand drive, then perhaps it is best left alone. Vantage cars were not specially identified on the chassis.

Engine numbers will be found on the main chassis plate and also stamped on the forward nearside of the engine block. The stamp will read something like 370/958 – 370 for a 3.7 engine, 958 for its number. The engines were not mated to particular cars, but generally the engine and chassis numbers will approximate to each other. A car with a chassis number in the high 900s should not have an engine in the low 700s, for example.

The only designation of a Vantage model is the use of the SS suffix on the engine block number, not the head. The presence of three carburettors on the head is not a guarantee of a Special Series engine, as the process of putting three, rather than two, manifolds on the head is very straightforward. The presence of three SUs rather than two, in fact, will hardly affect the performance. Given that all blocks are the same casting, this is quite important. At any rate, a 3.7-litre cylinder head should at least have single domed nuts holding the cam covers on. The use of double nuts indicates that the head is a 4-litre – but a very few 4-litre engines used single nuts, such as some fitted to the Lagonda Rapide. If you are looking at a cylinder head casting, with no valve gear attached, the 4-litre is distinguishable from the 3.7-litre by the presence of a 2mm chamfer running around the rim of each combustion chamber. This was done to mate the chamber to the cylinder bore on the later engines. The valve seats can also be measured to determine whether they are of Special Series and 4-litre dimension or regular DB4 size. If the engine is dismantled and incomplete, this is a good way to tell.

A GT head, of course, has twin ignition and Special Series size valves. Fifteen DB4s of the 1112 made (this total includes the two prototypes) had GT engines, while 70 cars were convertibles. The use of the 'five series' approach to DB4 production reveals the following breakdown:

Two prototypes. DP184/1 and DP184/2; 1956 and 1957.

Series One. DB4/101/R – DB4/250/L; October 1958 to February 1960; 149 cars made, all saloons.

Series Two. DB4/251/L – DB4/600/R; January 1960 to April 1961; 249 cars made, all saloons.

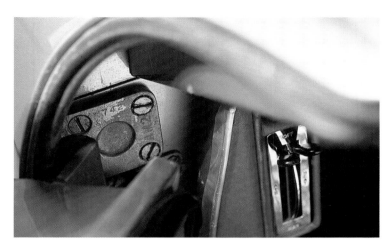

The chassis number on the door hinge: 742 means Series 3.

The identification plate found on the right of the engine bay. The body number will be found to be the same as the chassis number. The practice of numbering body and chassis separately was dropped with the fourth series of DB4.

Series Three. DB4/601/R – DB4/765/R; April 1961 to September 1961; 164 cars made, all saloons.

Series Four. DB4/766/R – DB4/1080/R; September 1961 to October 1962; 314 cars made, 30 convertibles, 284 saloons.

Series Five. DB4/1081/L – DB4/1215/L; September 1962 to June 1963; 134 cars made, 40 convertibles, 94 saloons.

Convertibles used sequential chassis numbers from DB4C1051/R to DB4C1110/L and then DB4C1166/R to DB4C1175/L, effectively straddling the Series Four/Five changeover. A total of 32 convertibles had Special Series engines and one had a GT engine, this and one of the Special Series engined cars having a faired-in front end.

A total of 136 saloon cars in Series Four and Five had Vantage engines, while 11 saloons had the GT engine. Most, but not all, of the Special Series engined cars used the faired-in front. Records are inexact as to how many DB4s were given Special Series

cylinder heads after being sold, but the option cost significantly less than automatic transmission!

There are, of course, always the funny ones. The DB5 with the DB4 front, for example, or the standard DB4 with the faired-in lights. Several cars will be found with 4-litre engines, or at least 4-litre heads, and they are probably better cars for it. Some will have ZF gearboxes, as well, but these things do not pose huge problems in identification.

If, after the foregoing, there is still a problem in properly identifying your car or one you are offered, I can only recommend contacting Aston Service Dorset. For a small contribution to a worthy cause, they will find the original factory build sheet and send you a copy. It will also give you the great pleasure of dealing with them. The build sheet provides virtually all the information you could conceivably want, and a little more besides. Be prepared to find out, though, that after at least 28 years, your car may not look now the way it did when new.

The DB4 GT

DB4GT. This car is still actively campaigned on the racetrack.

Most superlatives within the lexicon of excellence have already been used to describe this car, and this is not really the place for any more. Basically, it is a shortened, lightened DB4 with an engine tuned to the existing limits of reliability. It was not a racing car, although the prototype, DP199, first appeared in that role before the model was officially launched at the 1959 motor show, a year after the introduction of the DB4. Clearly, the advantages and disciplines of the Superleggera method of construction could be applied in an even more ambitious manner than they had already been despite the teething troubles that the production car was having. The combination of a 28% increase in power, 16% more torque and 185lb less weight created a car which simply staggered those who drove it. It still does.

The weight lost was actually rather less than one might have thought, given the changes made to the chassis. The platform is shortened by 5in in front of the rear wheels, at the area of the rear jacking point. This is most noticable when looking at the doors, which are discernibly abbreviated. The rear seats are sacrificed, the space being used for luggage. Most of the boot is occupied by an enlarged tank, on top of which sits the spare wheel. The front/rear weight distribution is 51%/49%, unchanged from the DB4.

The chassis, then, is modified by shortening it, thus reducing its weight, rather than by the lightening of the specifications of the materials used in its fabrication. Length apart, it closely resembles the DB4 chassis and follows its method of construction exactly. Given that the platform is shortened inside the wheelbase, the structure is even more rigid than that of the standard car. The rear seat support pan is lost and the Superleggera cage has a slightly changed profile in order to support the shorter roof. Otherwise, the methods and materials used are identical. Certain of the lightweight cars produced by the works used a large amount of aluminium in the chassis to replace steel parts which were unstressed in the original design, but these were an exception to the rule. Many of these lightening techniques are to be seen in the modified club racing classes today.

The front suspension is identical, down to front spring deflection rates and angle settings. The rear suspension is broadly the same, using the same geometry, except that the rear springs are much more compliant. Their free length is increased to 15³/₄in, they use 10¹/₂ coils instead of 9, and have a

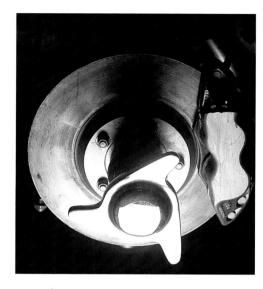

The Girling brake layout first used on the DB4GT was later phased into the DB5 with the addition of a servo.

deflection rate of 110lb/in, as opposed to 132lb/in.

Steering uses the same type of Aston Martin rack, with gearing unchanged at 2.8 turns lock to lock. Owing to the shorter wheelbase, the turning circle is reduced to 32ft from 34ft.

The brakes are totally different, and made by Girling, rather than Dunlop. The calipers used are Girling type C with a 2³/₈in caliper cylinder bore at the front and 1¹¹/₁₆in at the rear. The discs at the front have a 12.06in diameter at the front and are 0.605in thick; at the rear the diameter is 11in, the thickness .418in. The swept area is 499sq in. Two master cylinders are used, each of ⁵/₈in bore, one acting on the front brakes, the other on the rear. The pressure is regulated by a balance bar between the two cylinders and each has its own reservoir, these being located on the main bulkhead on the offside in a RHD car. There is no servo unit on a DB4GT, the space being used by the reservoirs. The two master cylinders also act to support each other, using the balance regulator, should one cylinder fail. The same handbrake mechanism is used as on DB4 models up to chassis 600.

The rear axle is unchanged from the DB4, save for the addition of the Powr-Lok limited-slip differential as standard on all ratios, as opposed to the optional status this equipment has on the DB4. The same final drives are offered − the 4.09 axle is the lowest, 2.93 the highest − and allow the same spread of direct-drive maxima as on the DB4.

The wheels are invariably alloy Borrani centre lock wires, with 72 steel spokes and triple-eared spinners. They have 5¹/₂in rims

This, I suppose, is the ultimate DB4, a Zagato-bodied GT. This car, which now belongs to Richard Williams, was owned by Dr Zagato. It is unique in being the only example to have an air scoop on the bonnet. When first announced, it was described by John Bolster as looking 'fierce beyond belief'. It still does.

From the rear there is just a small hint, around the rear quarterlight, of the DB6 to come.

clutch, rather than the other way around.

The body, after all these similarities, is rather different. It is still made using the Superleggera system, but the outer alloy skin is of 18swg and, in certain individual cars, even 20swg, 'just to keep the rain off', as it were. Thus the key principle of wrapping a steel frame in a lightweight alloy body is kept, although both the frame and the body are marginally lighter.

Apart from the shortened doors, the most obvious difference between the GT and the standard car is the front headlight treatment, which introduces the cowled shape later seen on the DB4 Vantage. There are two types of cowl. One, seen on later cars, uses an aluminium rimmed perspex cover which is secured by means of four self-tapping screws. The other type, generally seen on earlier cars, has no rim and appears to be larger, although both types are the same size. On either type, the side lamp is moved inside the cover, leaving only the flasher lamp outside.

Bumpers on the DB4GT are generally without overriders, and usually of the intermediate type – heavier duty with no reflectors built into them. Tail lamps were of the same type as contemporary DB4s, so that the date of the car's construction tends to decide which type is used. Likewise with the bonnet scoop and the grille, the introduction of the fourth series of DB4 being the change period. Of course, several cars will have features from both earlier and later

models, acquired over the years. One aspect of the GT which is a carryover from the very early days of the DB4 is the absence of window frames, although the use of plexiglass in the rear quarterlights and rear light is unique to the GT. Otherwise, body fittings are the same for both models.

The interior of a DB4GT is similar in design to that of a DB4 – there is merely rather less of it. The same 'Vaumol' leather is used on the seats, the rake adjustment mechanism being a simple threaded stop, and these sit on the same carpet. Generally, there are no rear seats, although a few cars have tiny ones, for children only. As a rule, the space is taken up by a carpeted luggage

shelf. The headlining, along with its two recesses, is the same plastic material as before. The boot space, as mentioned, is occupied by a large fuel tank, on top of which sits the spare Borrani, held in place by a leather Y strap.

The dashboard of the GT is identifiable by the presence of many more gauges, but little more actual information. It is more readable, using none of the combination instruments of the DB4; the fuel and water temperature gauges are separate, as are the oil pressure and oil temperature gauges. The same instrument binnacle and steering wheel are used.

It is, then, a car which is obviously a

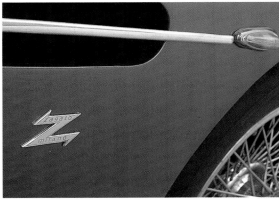

The interior is purposeful and distinctly Italianate. This particular car was supplied in chassis form to Zagato and bodied and trimmed in Milan.

Zagato GT boot, largely filled by the fuel tank and spare wheel, offers no improvement in space on the DB4GT's.

Zagato's trademark on the flank. The characteristic Aston Martin side vent was retained.

DB4, certainly lighter and faster, but just as substantial as the standard model. It is also very rare. Of the 100 cars manufactured, 74 were broadly to the specification above.

A further 19 cars were bodied by Zagato. These carry the same type designation (not GTZ) and were announced at the 1960 Motor Show, being greeted with unalloyed enthusiasm. All these cars are different, although the basic design was by one Ercole Spada, a Zagato house designer. Despite, or possibly because of, its rarity, this car seems to possess one of the highest 'recognition factors' of all Aston Martins, except possibly the DB5. It is, of course, quite wonderful to look at, bearing a close resemblance to

other, later, work by that company, particularly that done on the Lancia Flaminia. It is obviously a Zagato, lacking only the famous 'double bubble' roof, but equally obviously an Aston Martin, the front end being an elegant caricature of the Aston grille. Recently, in mid-1991, four 'Sanction II' cars have been completed, by Zagato, on DB4GT chassis, using numbers originally unallocated by Aston Martin. To describe the Zagato model in detail is unnecessary here, except to say that it uses a standard DB4 GT chassis and the 314bhp engine mentioned above. Five cars were completed and trimmed in Italy, the balance being shipped back to the UK for finishing.

Of the seven cars remaining after the Zagatos are added to the list, the last chassis was bodied by Bertone, elegantly but with much adornment, and there were four DB4GT inspired 'Project cars', which used high-output variants of the GT engine in various capacities. Finally, there were two development prototypes.

The DB4GT is the car which comes closest to the character of some of the exotic 250 Ferraris, against which it indeed competed. Weight was generally slightly against it, however, but many have found great success in club racing over the years, despite their ever-increasing value. However, as one exponent pointed out to me some time ago, cost of repair is only a handicap when a car is not worth much.

The DB4 Convertible

All 70 of the DB4 convertibles made are Series 4/5 cars. The conversion is particularly handsome.

This is a car which truly confirms that the DB4 is styled by Touring of Milan, despite the fact that the redesign was done in-house at Aston Martin. Anyone who has seen the Lancia Flaminia drophead which that firm designed already knows what a DB4 Convertible looks like. Possibly the prettiest car ever built by Aston Martin, this is a rarer car than the DB4GT, only 70 having been made, all of them in the fourth and fifth series. The profile of the car adopts the same basic design, unavoidable when removing the roof of a fastback, as the DB2/4 series – a longer boot is introduced and rear head-room is improved somewhat.

The convertible uses the same basic chassis as the saloon, with some additional strength-ening in order to compensate for the lack of a roof cage. The sills are stiffened internally, as is the area under the rear seat pan and the recess for the folded hood frame, necessitat-ing the use of two eight gallon tanks, one in each wing – this was arguably not enough. Evidence suggests that the bodies of these cars invariably crack at the rear threequarter panel, due to the proximity of the fuel filler flaps to both the boot hinge and the rear cabin surround. Restorers usually undertake some redesigning in this area, so that the body itself takes less of the stress, by the

The side profile with hood raised is pleasing. The hardtop, when fitted, follows the same general profile.

expedient of reinforcing the B-posts inter-nally and adding more stiffening across the 'pelvis' of the car, behind the rear seat. Obviously, even with this extra support, the rear of the platform has greater loads than before placed upon it, due to the structure not having the benefit of the roof cage, but a reasonable compromise is reached. Perhaps it is only right and proper that some sacrifice should be made in order to enjoy this style of bodywork.

The mechanical characteristics of the DB4 Convertible (under no circumstances should

Convertible seen from the Members' Bridge at Brooklands. This is one of the 17 cars built using the longer body from the fifth series. Chassis number DB4C 1084/R, it was originally the works demonstrator, but is now owned by Paul Dobson, spares registrar of the AMOC, membership of which should really be compulsory if you consider acquiring one of these cars.

The convertible dashboard is painted body colour but the layout is the same as on the saloon.

this be called a Volante) are entirely the same as for the saloon: the only differences are to be found in the bodywork and interior. Wheel size follows the trend of the saloon model, with either 16in or 15in Dunlop wires or the Borrani option. Whereas the saloon body is made in two sections, the rear one comprising everything aft of the screen rail, the convertible rear section starts at the B-post. The rear hood support is a steel fabrication, around which the rear shroud is clenched. Aft of the B-post, as on the saloon, the edges of the body are wired, placing the wheelarches and the rear skirt under tension. The bootlid is longer, being a simple curve. Whether the car is from the fourth or fifth series, it will be of the appropriate length – all but 17 cars have the shorter Series Four body length. But on all cars the screen is deeper, adding 1in to the height of the car, the top corners of the screen being squared off to allow the use of slim screen pillars. Quarterlights are used, to prevent the hood 'ballooning' at high speed, and the unframed window glasses are thus shortened, the doors being the same overall length. The hood is erected manually, using a frame of Aston Martin design, not dissimilar to the frame found on a DB MkIII.

A hardtop was introduced for the fifth series cars, although theoretically it will fit both series four and DB5 models, and is lined with the headlining material used in the saloon. Opinions differ as to its elegance, but it seems to be a totally logical shape.

The convertible's long boot lid. From this angle, this car could easily be mistaken for a DB5 convertible.

The interior is similar in design to the DB4, but the rear seat is modified, the back being more upright, and the cushion shorter. The padded hood bag is leather. The folding top is covered in 'Everflex' material, although cars retrimmed at the factory can be seen with mohair tops. Originally the tonneau cover, if fitted, is vinyl, fastened with press studs at the dash top and door caps. The dashboard is generally of DB4 style, although some cars have GT instrument binnacles. The dash itself is either body colour or black, as in the saloon.

The DB4 Convertible, then, is an extremely rare and elegant car. Examples will frequently be found with lower axle ratios than standard, due to the impracticality of cruising at the high speeds offered by

the highest final drives; 3.77:1 seems to be the most common, although the default ratio remained 3.54:1.

The DB4 Convertible really completes the study of the DB4 as a separate model. Clearly, all variants and derivatives have a great deal in common, both in terms of their construction and the engineering philosophy and quality which went into their design and manufacture. As an interesting exercise, it is useful to subject the DB4's contemporary Italian-built rivals to the same level of scrutiny. As one unavoidably realises that the build quality of the Aston is simply superior, particularly in the chassis and body, to a Maserati or a Ferrari, then one concludes that perhaps the best skills of Italian design were employed in the export trade.

Lagonda Rapide

It is hard to understand why two contemporaneous vehicles, of broadly similar mechanical specification and produced by the same company, should have come to be regarded with hindsight in such different ways. The DB4 has achieved the status of a true milestone in post-war car design. The Lagonda Rapide, on the other hand, has been variously dismissed, derided or merely ignored. This is perplexing, to say the least.

David Brown had done little with Lagonda in terms of redeveloping the marque, with the exception of the rather overbodied Tickford models, and wished to establish for it an identity of its own. The demise of the Tickford Lagonda 3-litre, propelled by the larger manifestation of the LB6 engine, had been a disappointment to David Brown, the more so because it had been preceded by a cut in the price by £1000. This tactic was to have more success when used to sell unsold DB6 stock ten years later. The decision to develop the Rapide model on a modified version of the DB4 chassis was Brown's alone and was one which was to cause some difficulties.

Back to project 114. This prototype was a contemporary of the 3-litre Lagonda – indeed it used the same engine. A feature which set it apart from existing models had

been the use of a de Dion system at the back, using experience gained during the racing programme. DP114, though, was a comparatively light car, whereas the purpose of reviving the Lagonda marque was to introduce a larger sports saloon more along the lines of the Jaguar models. The reduction in unsprung weight offered by the use of the de Dion axle, coupled with increased space in the back, was an irresistible attraction. It was known that the layout worked well, on racing cars at least, and would go a long way to correcting certain handling deficiences which would otherwise result from stretching the DB4 platform.

Stretched it certainly was. The wheelbase of the Rapide was increased by 16in to 114in, and the weight went up by almost 1000 pounds, as did the price. The chassis was altered at the rear in order to secure the mounting of the de Dion layout, in which the final drive is bolted via insulation pads, directly to the chassis itself. This is all well and good, except that vibration can pass into the chassis under certain circumstances. Due to the fact that the drive shafts coming out of the final drive were angled forward about 1in, those circumstances were present. Rapid wear of the splines was the result. It is this feature of the Rapide which is often

In styling terms the Rapide almost makes it from the front, its sheer presence making up for the slightly baroque nose. The original Touring design called for a DB4 style of headlamp – to rebuild one that way might be nice, but given that the car is three inches wider, it would be rather more complicated than grafting on a DB4 front end.

From the rear, the exercise is much more successful. This is how Touring designed it. It resembles both the DB4 drophead and the contemporary SIII Continental Rolls/Bentley.

cited for its unpopularity, very often by those who have never driven one. It can be noisy, for sure, but I fondly remember the Rapide I owned, albeit briefly, being wonderfully smooth and chuckable.

The front suspension is as for the DB4, using the same spring rates. The steering is lower-geared than on the DB4, an extra half-turn being needed to explore both extremes of lock. The turning circle of 42 ft is a function of the extra length. Brakes are Dunlop disc, as on the DB4, with the same Girling servo unit. The final drive offered a choice of 3.77:1 or 3.54:1, as within the differential were the same Salisbury gears as before. As people were to find with the automatic DB6, the 3.77 ratio left the car rather undergeared in automatic form. Wheels and tyres were rather different, although the hubs used are the same. They now carry pressed steel 15in Dunlop wheels shod with 7.10 x 15 Avon Turbospeeds. It is not thought that wire wheels were offered.

Mechanically, the Rapide was offered with either the DB4 Special Series engine, or a 3995cc unit of the same dimensions as the DB5 and 6 engine, the bores being increased to 96mm. Cams are standard DB4 intervals. The appearance of the engine bay is the same, except that some 4-litre units still used single cam cover bolts as opposed to paired ones. Torque was improved to 260lb ft but power output was unchanged, albeit at a lower peak.

The cooling system is also identical to the other models. Air conditioning, by

Normalair, was an option, with the pattern as on the DB5. The exhaust system set the trend for the 4-litre models, using four Burgess silencers of a straight-through type.

The fuel system uses a pair of fuel tanks, located in each rear wing. Access is via electrically operated filler flaps set either side of the leading edge of the bootlid. The pump, the same SU type, draws from both tanks. Carburettors are either the Solex PHH 44 two-stage type, which use an accelerator pump cutting in at a predetermined engine speed, or the triple SU set-up from the DB4 Special Series. The former, which are also found on the Mercedes 190SL and the Alfa Romeo 2600, are unobtainable now, but few will mourn their passing. They are die-cast items which are prone to cracking, and overhaul is massively expensive. With other applications of this carburettor, there is a Weber replacement, but two twin-choke single-stage carburettors on a six-cylinder engine might give tuning difficulties.

The transmission will either be a Borg Warner automatic with a speed hold, or the S432 David Brown four-speed manual as on the DB4. Both transmissions are described elsewhere.

Electrically, the car follows the established pattern. Lucas provide everything, except for a few lights inside and the dreaded Piper electric windows. Demisting fans on the rear parcel shelf were an optional extra.

There is another reason for the car having received a bad press over time – the styling. For most people, the only reservations about

the Rapide's appearance concern the front, where it would appear that the work was carried out by the styling department at Metro-Cammell. The rest of the car has rather pleasing proportions, particularly when compared to the rather whale-like Jaguar Mk10, which was a contemporary. There is at least one Rapide running around with a DB4 radiator grille of the later type, but this was merely an attempt to bring the vehicle more obviously into the David Brown family and was possibly a post-production modification. It is described in an encyclopaedia of British cars as having a special body, possibly because it was the property of the author of that publication. However, beauty is in the eye of the beholder and the styling is really no more extravagent than that of the 'Chinese Eye' Rolls model or the Jensen C-V8, the latter being a car which has gained a certain popularity despite its looks and rear suspension.

The construction of the body follows established practice, but there is rather more of it. The Rapide's body is 18in longer than the DB4's and, of course, has four small doors. The extra length is in the boot overhang. The roof cage is more substantial, having many more transverse members, and the pillar is much strengthened. The same practice of fabricated steel apertures is followed, and the body itself is of 16swg aluminium alloy as before. It is, apart from the front end, an extremely elegant, balanced car, easily as attractive from the side as many of the offerings from specialist builders

on Rolls or Bentley chassis. The rear end is reminiscent of the DB4 drophead or the Mulliner Bentley S3, using as it does the same type of rear lamps as the Series Three/Four DB4. The bumpers are lengthened versions of the later DB4 type, the whole car being 3in wider.

The interior is amazing. There are two styles, one following DB4 practice, the other rather reminiscent of the previous Lagondas. The first style uses the upholstery pattern of the DB4 on the seats and a DB4 instrument binnacle. A slightly odd touch is a quilted leather transmission tunnel cover. Picnic tables are built into the rears of the front seats, which are substantially padded *à la* Mercedes-Benz. Otherwise, headlining is West of England cloth (with no head recesses) and carpet is Wilton.

The second style is more luxurious, the seats having horizontal pleats in them rather than vertical, and the dash panel being of

wood. The instruments, from the DB4, are arranged in line in a shallow cowl, which is echoed on the passenger side. The steering wheel is either DB4 or a slightly dished type. Either way, the DB motif remains, but set into red plastic rather than blue. The boot is massive and lined with black carpet.

Overall, the Rapide is an extraordinary car, but one which really fell between two stools. On the one hand, the competition was Jaguar with its Mk2 and Mk10 saloons, and on the other it was Bentley. Alvis cars were pitched at around the same market, as were the better Mercedes models. The Lagonda was also ferociously expensive. Perhaps people felt that this was too much a badge-engineered Aston and a little too Italianate for its market. Whatever they thought, it was, and is, a fine car. Given the choice between a Rapide and an automatic DB6, I think that it might be a very close call indeed.

The Rapide's interior offers a level of splendour acceptable to the most cosseted backside, whether owner-driver or chauffeur. This is the second style of interior, with wood dash and horizontally-pleated seats. The quality of appointments in the rear compartment speaks for itself.

The DB5

From the rear, the DB5 is the same as a late DB4. The raised roofline and extra body length force the roofline to converge differently with the boot. It is a more powerful car than the early DB4, but needs to be. Its weight has now grown by a whopping 450lbs.

Work order 24084, dated 5 December 1962 and issued by John Wyer, called for a '4-litre Aston Martin DB4' to be coded DP 216. It was to have a 4-litre triple SU engine, an oil cooler, a Borg & Beck 9in or 9½in clutch, an S432 gearbox with overdrive, a 3.77:1 axle, electric windows, a radio, Sundym glass and fog lamps. It was to be silver grey, with grey leather and grey carpets.

Shortly afterwards, this very car would be seen, loaded with improbable gadgetry, in the Eon Films production of *Goldfinger* by Ian Fleming. To this day, it remains a mystery as to why Sean Connery had to drive the car without sun visors, but I am sure that someone knows the answer. Despite this mystery, the film no doubt aided the sales of the model, well over 1000 being produced.

This transition from DB4 to DB5 is an almost imperceptible one in terms of the car's appearance. The last few cars of the Series Five DB4 Vantage finalised the looks of the DB5 model by the addition of twin petrol filler flaps, the extra one being let into the nearside rear screen pillar. It had been evident that the DB4 Vantage was felt to be such an impressive car by the road testers who drove it and the owners who bought it

that the gap between the DB4 and the DB4GT was now much less than before. Thus, the DB5 had become the only Aston Martin model available by the time of its introduction in the summer of 1963, the GT having been discontinued. It is generally held that the DB5 finally conquered the development problems which had dogged the DB4, but in fact the DB4 had already become, in its later manifestations, a perfectly reliable vehicle.

The DB5 has a different front, too, similar to the GT and DB4 Vantage. This car has the later chromed headlamp cowl trims.

CHASSIS

Little time need be spent describing the chassis of the DB5, for it is almost exactly the same as the fifth series of the preceding model, using the 98in wheelbase. One small difference, though, is the deletion of the separate alloy ball joint socket for the brake reaction arm, this now being integral with the chassis.

After chassis 1340, however, a small change was made to accommodate the five-speed ZF gearbox which became standard, the David Brown unit being applied prior to that. The pedal box was also modified to accept the new casting on which the brake and clutch master cylinders are mounted. Otherwise, the materials and methods are the same as for the DB4.

FRONT SUSPENSION

The front suspension geometry is the same, except that the kingpin inclination is now 5½ degrees and the maximum camber angle now 1 degree. The method of locating the lower wishbone brake reaction arm, though, is modified and, from the point of view of the restorer, much improved. Gone is the potentially troublesome aluminium ball joint retainer, replaced by a socket integral with the chassis. Overhaul (and restoration) is thus simplified. The ball joint itself is unchanged, being common to all cars. The steering system is also identical.

REAR SUSPENSION

At the rear, the DB4 set-up is still used, and the Armstrong 'Selectaride' is still optional. Otherwise, dampers and springs are as on the DB4.

BRAKES

The DB5's brakes are different, being a development of the Girling system used on the DB4GT. In the case of the DB5, however, the balance mechanism employed on the DB4GT is absent because only one master cylinder is used; but twin Girling Mk2A servos are fitted, the front brakes working from the offside unit, the rears from the nearside. On Vantage models, a vacuum reservoir is fitted in front of the offside B-post and can be reached by removing the stone guard behind the front wheel. This is a good way of verifying the authenticity of a 'Webered' car.

Selectaride adjustable rear dampers are optional, as on the later DB4 models. The switch which operates them resembles a gas cooker control and sits at the bottom left of the instrument panel.

The front suspension is similar to the DB4, but the brakes are now by Girling, this make having been fitted to the DB4GT previously. For ease of operation, twin servos have been added.

The front brake calipers are fitted with triple cylinders, using two of 1.59in bore and one of 2.25in. The rear brakes use more modest equipment, namely two 1.19in and one 1.68in wheel cylinders. The master cylinder is of ⅞in bore. Disc diameters are 11½in at the front and 10¾in at the rear; total swept area is 468sq in. Twin reservoirs are mounted on the main bulkhead, the container for the rear brakes doubling as a clutch reservoir.

The calipers employ a similar set-up to

There are now two Girling 2A servos, as opposed to Dunlop, one on each side of the engine bay. The correct finish is gloss black.

Here are the 72-spoke 15in wheels inherited from the late DB4, in this case chromed. Borrani wheels remained an option.

the DB4GT, in order to equalise the pressure between the separate wheel cylinders. On the front calipers, the casting is internally drilled to allow fluid to spread evenly. On the rears, a separate bridge pipe is used, located on the top of the caliper. Despite the reduced swept area compared to the DB4, the brakes are much improved, due partly to the greater degree of vacuum assistance and partly to the improved caliper design.

It is not uncommon to find DB5 brakes grafted on to DB4s at the front, but generally without the extra servo unit. If a DB5 is found to have Dunlop brakes fitted, it is either not a DB5 at all, or it has been fundamentally interfered with, probably to save money. The DB5 uses the same braking system throughout its production without any modification. Appearence is as for the DB4, with the exception of the servos, which are painted black.

REAR AXLE

The DB5's rear axle is the same Salisbury 4HA. Two previously optional ratios, the 2.93:1 and the 4.09:1 at opposite ends of the spectrum, are deleted, leaving 3.33:1, 3.54:1 and 3.77:1. The first becomes the default ratio for four-speed models, with 3.54:1 as an option. For four-speed overdrive models, 3.77:1 becomes the option. Five-speed models usually have the 3.77:1 axle as standard. Powr-Lok differentials are optional on all ratios. On a few later five-speed models, the 3.77:1 axle was supplanted by a 3.73:1

ratio, which was to become the default setting on manual DB6 cars. On automatic cars, the default ratio remains the same as the DB4, at 3.54:1.

WHEELS & TYRES

The equipment remains the same as on the Series Five DB4: the 15in Dunlop wheels have 72 spokes and a 5¹⁄₂in rim. Tyres are crossply, by Avon or Dunlop. Borrani wheels were optional, but used the same tyres.

ENGINE

There are some fairly obvious differences here. The block casting is the same as the DB4, but machined to accept liners of a bigger bore, 96mm, to give a new displacement of 3995cc. The crankshaft is the same steel forging as before, the throw being unchanged, but the shaft is no longer Nitrided. Bearing sizes are the same, for both big ends and mains. The oil pump is of the same type as the DB4 and the sump is of the last DB4 type, with a capacity of 21

The DB5 engine is similar in appearance to the Special Series DB4, but note the paired cam cover studs and the strengthening ribs. The green plug leads are correct. The carburettor dashpot tops are now plastic. There are in fact two bonnet props.

The exhaust side. Note the correct type of air trunking.

pints, to which is added the two pints held in the oil cooler – now, at long last, a standard item. The oil pressure should still be around the same as the 3.7-litre engine at around 100lb/sq in at 3000rpm.

The cylinder head casting is the same as the 3.7 engine, except that the combustion chamber is chamfered, to allow it to mate with the bigger bore of the liners – it sounds primitive! The rationale, though, is that the chamber cannot be reworked fully without changing its internal hemispherical section, to the detriment of its efficiency. The use of the chamfer allows a gas-tight fit and maintains the inherently effective shape of the chamber. That is my story, and I am sticking to it – but a few eyebrows may justifiably be raised at the discovery of this practice.

The pistons are still die-cast alloy, but now use three compression rings and an oil-control ring. The valves are of the same diameter as those of the DB4 Special Series engine, namely 2in and 1.875in for inlet and exhaust respectively. Seats and seat angles are the same as before. Cam timing changes: the inlet now opens at 17 degrees BTDC and closes at 79 degrees ABDC; the exhaust opens at 69 degrees BBDC and closes at 23 degrees ATDC. Valve adjustment follows previous practice.

The appearance of the engine is basically similar, but there are detailed differences. The cam covers are now secured with paired studs along their length, as opposed to single ones, and strengthening ribs are added to them, to prevent oil leaks. The crankcase breathers remain where they are

for late 3.7 engines, but timing covers are not interchangeable between these engines, due to the presence of a damper which is attached to a modified timing cover casting. Porting is the same, so that the manifolds, finished as before, are interchangeable. The DB5 has triple bifurcated manifolds, whatever the specification of the engine. Power output is raised only mildly over the DB4 Special Series, to 282bhp at 5500rpm and 280lb ft of torque at 4500rpm – note that peak torque arrives a little later in the 4-litre engine than on the 3.7.

Vantage tune for the DB5 is no longer referred to as Special Series. The engine number will be suffixed by a simple V, the chassis number not at all. Vantage tune was initially referred to as 'GT' specification at design stage, but re-named for production. Unlike the DB4, some change is made in cam timing on these engines, albeit not as radically as on the GT version. In Vantage tune, the inlet opens at 29 degrees BTDC and closes at 67 degrees ABDC, while the exhaust opens at 58 degrees BBDC and closes at 34 degrees ATDC. Compression is

This rear end shot shows the extra silencers and the rear axle location.

raised to 8.9:1 and Weber carburettors are employed instead of the standard DB5's triple SU HD8s taken from the DB4 Vantage. Power is raised to 314bhp at 5500rpm and torque to 290lb ft at 4500rpm.

It had been Aston Martin's intention to supply twin ignition for the Vantage engine: this was an established practice by now, but, as rebuilders have discovered, the increased valve diameters in an unmodified combustion chamber make the addition of an extra plug a little difficult. Cracking of the head between valve seats on the 3.7 GT and the 4-litre has been an occasional problem over time. The benefits in terms of simplicity and reliability have, I feel, outweighed the rather marginal advantage of twin ignition.

The bulk of the 21% increase in torque between the standard DB4 and the DB5 Vantage is cancelled out by a 12.5% increase in weight. Given that the torque peaks a little later on the DB5, acceleration figures in the mid-ranges are little different, but above 80mph the improvements become clear. All in all, the detail improvements in the 4-litre engine add up to a more flexible unit with huge top end power. There was little improvement in torque over the DB5 Vantage engine during the rest of the production life of the unit, although power output crept up a little. Altogether, only 65 DB5s received the Vantage engine.

COOLING SYSTEM

Broadly, the system used on the DB4 is retained, without the radiator blind. On cars up to chassis 1526, an electric engine fan is used, operated by a thermostat switch which opens at around 85 degrees C. Subsequently, the eight-blade fan from the DB4 was reintroduced. Either way, a Ferodo V4999 belt is used.

The DB5's system is probably no better than the DB4's. The Serck radiator, with five rows of tubing, seems not to be up to the task. Modifications can be made, one being to reduce the size of the bypass at the pump to allow more water actually to pass through the radiator. There is also enough space to install a radiator with a denser core within the overall dimensions of the casing. Anecdotal evidence of overheating difficulties on all DB4, 5 and 6 Astons is strong enough to suggest that this is a reasonable idea, at least for high-speed driving. More on this in the restoration section. Originality, in the concours sense, is all about appearance, after all, rather than engineering.

The water pump, predictably, is the same as before, as is the thermostat range. The appearance of the components is unchanged; the Kenlowe electric fan is in the manufacturer's finish.

EXHAUST SYSTEM

This is rather more complicated – but more 'civilized' – than the DB4's. The basic layout, including heat shields, is the same, but the DB5 uses four Burgess silencers instead of two. Back pressure, of course, is increased. Some DB5s will be found with a DB4 system; the reverse is seldom true. Again, 16 swg mild steel is original. The extra silencers are behind the flexible section on the front pipes.

CARBURETTORS & FUEL SYSTEM

In standard form, the DB5 uses the Special Series arrangement from the DB4 of triple SU HD8 carburettors. They are identical instruments, although UU needles are specified, replaced by UX. Again, some experimentation should be tried to adjust for modern fuels. Generally, the dashpot tops would be black plastic by 1963, but not invariably. As before, a black-painted cold air box is used, with a Purolator MF19215 filter and an MF192 paper element. This will often be absent, discarded either through negligence or a naive search for greater power at the expense of quietness.

The Vantage engine tune has Weber

Twin fuel fillers are now standard.

The ZF five-speed gear change, used from chassis 1340.

The DB5's battery now lives here, under the rear seat. The same isolator switch is still used, and the battery is of 60a/h capacity instead of 51a/h.

45DCOE9 carburettors using a 40mm choke, in the same layout as used on the DB4GT. The original settings were as follows; main jet, 150; air correction jet, 125; accelerator pump, 55; idling jet, 55F6; and needle valve, 200. They use a similar cold air box and the same air filter.

The fuel filter, in either engine tune, is a line type, Purolator 47300B. Both types of carburettor also contain their own strainers.

The fuel tank is as before, but with an extra filler neck, as described. The SU fuel pump, of the same type, no longer doubles as a road sweeper, and is more sensibly mounted on the offside chassis longeron top, out of harm's way.

TRANSMISSION

Four types of transmission may be found on the DB5. The first two are the same as the late DB4 – a David Brown S432 four-speed box, with or without overdrive. The internal ratios for this box are as for the 'wide ratio' DB4 box. If overdrive is used it is of

the late DB4 type, with a reduction of 0.82:1, used with a 3.77:1 axle, providing a final ratio in overdrive top of 3.09:1.

From chassis 1340, the third option – a ZF S5 325 five-speed box with an overdrive top – will be found. Its internal ratios are: fifth, 0.834:1; fourth, 1:1; third, 1.23:1; second, 1.76:1; first, 2.70:1; reverse, 3.31:1. Thus, acceleration in reverse is appreciably quicker than before. There are no variations on these ratios.

From 1964, the Borg Warner Model 8 automatic transmission was offered as an extra, although not many owners opted for it. The highest ratio it offers is 1:1. It is described in greater detail in the chapter covering the DB6 model.

Most DB5s will be found with the ZF box, and opinion differs as to whether it is a better option than the David Brown unit. It is possibly more reliable, but certainly noisier when healthy. The overdrive top helps, of course, but the change is probably more awkward. As for the Borg Warner automatic, it finds few fans, at least on this

type of car.

The clutch is the same for the David Brown box or the ZF unit. It is no longer the Borg & Beck type as used on the DB4s, but rather a 10in Laycock diaphragm single-plate device. Some DB4s also will be found to have been fitted with this clutch.

ELECTRICAL EQUIPMENT & LAMPS

The differences here are minor but important. The battery capacity is increased, for reasons which will become clear, from 51 amp/hr to 60amp/hr – it is now a Lucas BV11A. Its location also changes, moving from the rear offside wing to a fabricated box under the rear seat – the position where a DB4 with air conditioning had its battery.

Coupled with the larger battery is a more powerful generator, a Lucas type 11AC alternator, positioned where the old dynamo lived. The same starter motor as before is used and the ignition equipment is the same

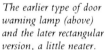

The earlier type of door warning lamp (above) and the later rectangular version, a little neater.

Earlier DB5s had alloy cowl trims similar to those of DB4GT. No DB4 used this chrome type.

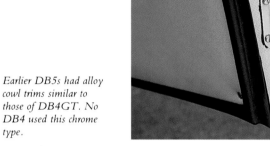

The DB5 gained a model badge, to distinguish it from a DB4. The car was announced mid-season, and rather slipped into production.

as for the Special Series DB4, although a DMBZ6 number 40981 distributor, with a marginally different advance curve, is quoted for late cars. Ignition timing is unchanged, although, like the carburettor settings, some experimentation is to be expected. The plug leads are of a suppressed type, coloured dark green instead of the original yellow and black. The black rubber terminals are the same, fitting vertically on the plug top. The finish of the engine ancillaries is as for the DB4 – either painted black or left in manufacturer's finish.

The windscreen wiper motor is now a Lucas 6W type (number 75445D), the wipers parking in front of the passenger. Electric window lifts are standard on the DB5, having been optional on the DB4. The motors were made by Piper, a firm no longer functioning – a quick assessment of the motor may reveal why. It is not a waterproof unit, so its operating life must be considered finite. It can be repaired, or a replacement can be used with a little fiddling. Favourites include many types of American appliances, freely available in Europe now that American automobiles are enjoying the surge of popularity they have long deserved, or, failing that, a Lucas unit as used in Jaguar cars.

Selectaride dampers, as mentioned, remained optional on the DB5 and can still be overhauled. The basic damper is still the same unit as used on the original DB4 model.

Other equipment includes a Lucas 3TR alternator control, with a Lucas 6RA relay and a Lucas 420197 contact set. The starter solenoid is a Lucas 2ST (number 76497) and the signalling relay, now of two-level intensity, is a Lucas 11RA. Door warning lamps are now fitted, of Lucas type 750 (number 56098B). Otherwise, all is the same as a DB4. The headlamp units are either Lucas F700, or Marchal A1411. Tail lamps are as fitted to the DB4 from Series Four onwards.

If fitted, the air conditioning unit is manufactured by Normalair. The condenser is mounted ahead of the radiator, the compressor being belt-driven via a solenoid clutch. The rest of the components are in the boot, necessitating the use of twin fuel tanks in each rear wing, of the same type as used on the DB4 Convertible. Fuel tank load is thus reduced, from 19 gallons, as with the DB4 saloon, to 16 gallons. If any other air conditioning system has been fitted, it is not original. Some cars will have had modern systems installed, and for reasons of comfort, given the heat soak from

the engine and exhaust, this is possibly a good idea. The advances made in the last 25 years in the technology of air conditioning are considerable, mainly in terms of the actual size of the components. The owner more concerned with comfort than originality has an opportunity, I think, to reap some benefits here.

BODY & BODY TRIM

The external appearance of the DB5 is indistinguishable from the final series of the DB4, even down to the twin filler flaps used on a few of the last examples of that car. The headlamp cowls are now standardised on the DB5, as opposed to being optional. At least one DB5, however, was built with the flat lamps as used on the DB4, and possibly there were more. It is hard to imagine that any were converted later in life to this appearance, although several DB4s have had cowled lamps fitted in order to 'update' their appearance.

From chassis 1609 and 1501, on saloons and convertibles respectively, external badges are to be found. One, on the offside of the bootlid, is of chromed Mazak lettering and two more, in front of the lower

The interior is still extremely relaxing, even if there is no extra room. Note the pleating of the rear seat; this pattern was introduced with the fifth series of DB4.

A-post on each side, have the lettering set into a black plastic badge, which is shield-shaped and rather cheap-looking. It is possible that this was done in answer to customer demand, for the DB5 was not launched with the same fanfare as its predecessor, being fed rather quietly into production during the summer prior to the motor show, with no external signs that it was a new model. It wasn't really one anyway, having no significant features which were completely new.

But there were a few insignificant ones. Warning lamps were at last fitted into the shut faces of the doors. These have a red lens and are operated by the same plunger switch as the interior lamps. Sundym glass became standard specification for all windows. On all DB5s apart from early cars (the change point is hard to determine), the headlamp cowl was modified from the alloy flush-fitting type to a rather more obtrusive chromed brass item, located at the top by a clip and at the bottom by a tab secured with a chromed screw. This type of cowl is used on the DB5 and DB6; although the DB4 lamp aperture can be modified to accept this later cover, a DB4 Vantage with cowled lamps was only ever fitted with the alloy type of cover. The sensible buyer might

remove the cover and search for any signs of plastic filler if he is inspecting what is advertised as a DB4 but finds the car wearing chromed lamp cowls.

INTERIOR

So far, then, the differences between the late DB4 and the DB5 are cosmetically negligible. Inside the car there are few more obvious changes. First, the door trims are new; the map pocket is now covered in vertical pleats to the front of the armrest, the scuff panel being the same. The ashtray is moved from behind the gear lever to in front of it on a five-speed car, because the ZF box is slightly longer than the David Brown type and leaves inadequate space in the old location. The transmission tunnel is lengthened for the ZF box. The ventilation controls on the A-posts are shuffled around, there now being one per side instead of the pair on the DB4; the missing ones are found on the facia panel. The seats are the same as late DB4 models but a chromed rib at the side is left exposed; earlier DB4s usually had this covered by hide, but there is some inconsistency here. The rear seat back is no longer pleated all the way across, now featuring six pleats on each side with a plain

The DB5 boot is lined in black carpet. Cars have been seen with Hardura boot trimmings, but some inconsistency is evident here.

The door trim panels are now pleated at the bottom.

centre section, echoing the pattern on the front seats. Carpets and headlining are as before, although the scuff panels either side of the transmission tunnel are now deleted.

DASHBOARD & INSTRUMENTS

The dashboard and binnacle are the same as the Series Five DB4 and GT, with some small changes.

The instrument bezels are flattened, instead of raised. The choke moves to a small chromed convex console under the clock, with the heater controls, and is now a slide control, like its companions. The electric window switches are moved from the doors to the space under the clock, where they become chromed rocker switches, displacing the pull switches which were previously there to the binnacle itself in toggle form, either side of the steering column. A choke warning lamp is fitted between the window lifts, while a brake fluid level warning lamp appears in the centre of the binnacle above the steering column. This depends for its operation on the buoyancy of the cork floats in the reservoirs; once buoyancy is lost through soaking, the light will stay on all the time, making night driving extremely tiresome. Some late DB4s were also fitted with this lamp. Apart from these items, the interior of the DB5 is identical to the late DB4.

As will be noted from the foregoing, the DB5 became a much more sophisticated car in terms of both creature comfort and performance delivery. For some reason, the DB4 is often referred to as being 'agricul-

tural' compared with the DB5. This description, I think, mainly concerns the gearbox and exhaust rather than anything else, for it is clear that there is little material difference between the two in other areas.

The engine gains power, to be sure, but the car also gains weight – some 350lb of it in standard form over the fourth series DB4. The 'softening' process which seems invariably to take place in the progression of the design of key models is clearly not absent here, but neither does it detract from the simply magnificent quality of the car.

The DB5 tool roll and jack. The touring tool kit offered by Raleigh Cycles is virtually identical.

The window switches, now electric as standard, move to the dash, above the choke. The choke control can be hard to find for the uninitiated, actually being the top slide above the heater controls.

The standard dash, evolved from the DB4GT type. This car has no Selectaride option.

IDENTIFICATION, DATING & PRODUCTION FIGURES

The DB5 had a relatively short life, between July 1963 and September 1965. The chassis numbering sequence began at 1251 and finished at 2275, more or less continuing from the previous DB4 numbers, which had ended at 1215. Of the total production of 1058, 123 were DB5 Convertibles and 37 were listed as DB6 Short Chassis Volantes. Of the remaining 898, 12 were converted to shooting brakes by Harold Radford and Co.

Within the overall series of chassis, there were four sequences of convertibles: chassis 1251–1300, 1501–1525, 1901–1925 and 2101–2123. The Short Chassis Volante, really a DB5 Convertible, used a group of numbers between DB5 and DB6, prefixed DBVC and running between 2301–2337.

A total of 65 cars were fitted with the Vantage engine, although it was not listed as a separate model. Check for the presence of the vacuum reservoir to confirm authenticity.

The DB5 Convertible

The DB5 Convertible was a logical develop-ment from the DB4 version. This is a rare Vantage model.

Again, like the DB4, the profile with the roof raised is logical and pleasing. Theoretically, the steel hardtop offered with the DB4 will fit the DB5 and short chassis DB6 cars as well.

The Short Wheelbase DB6 Volante (built on a DB5 chassis, of course), is very similar, apart from the rear lights, bumpers and badges. These cars are very rare, only 37 having been made. Making a virtue of necessity, as it were, for they were a means of using up spare DB5 chassis.

This is a model which seems to cause some confusion. Strictly speaking, a DB5 Convertible should not be referred to as a Volante – this term only applies to DB6 models. However, some DB Convertibles are really Volante convertibles, by virtue of the fact that they are built on DB5 chassis but included within DB6 production and called Short Wheelbase Volantes. I maintain that if a car is built on a DB5 chassis then it is really a DB5: the DB6 has distinct styling features and a different wheelbase. This may appear to be nit-picking on my part, but it seems more logical to include this model in the DB5 section than in the DB6, as the car is very much a DB5.

Basically, the DB5 Convertible follows all the modifications of the DB4 Convertible. Running modifications are as described for the saloon, and the adaptation of the chassis to accept drophead bodywork is also the same. There is one visual difference, which is the addition of extra flasher lamps on the sides of the car, forward of the wing vents. The same hardtop as used on the DB4 was an option on the DB5. There were four sequences of convertible by chassis number, the first being the lowest DB5 numbers of all.

The Volante model was an exercise undertaken to use up spare DB5 chassis after the model was no longer listed. Externally, the car is similar except for the rear lamps (which are from the DB6 saloon), the absence of the auxiliary flashers and the fact that only one type of headlamp cowl is used – the chrome plated one. The bumpers and interior are derived from the DB6 model, and will be described in the relevant section. The chassis is the same as for the DB5 Convertible.

The Triumph/DB6 type of rear lamp cluster as used on the Short Wheelbase Volante.

The Radford Estates

Every time you look again, you find a rarer one. This DB5 estate car was not, though, a Newport Pagnell product. Converted by Harold Radford from a saloon, it follows a logical, if dated, shape. For ease of operation, twin servos have been added.

The firm of Harold Radford carried out post-production estate body conversions on twelve DB5 saloons and seven DB6 saloons, the latter all prior to the introduction of the MkII. They were all basically similar in layout. Possibly the Leyland stylists – were there any then? – seized upon the DB6 estate as the inspiration for the rear end treatment of the Austin Allegro estate, but I cannot be sure. None of the cars were exactly the last word in elegance, but they were, even so, better-looking than any other contemporary estate cars – if rather less rigid than Aston Martin saloons.

In effect, a similar problem to the convertible cars was encountered in the sense that the Superleggera system, when used on a saloon car, provided great stiffness where all the tubing connected at the rear deck, converging back from the roof. As with the convertible, this was lost on the Radford cars, the extended roof almost fulfilling the function of the cage itself.

The DB5 roofline was flattened from the windscreen back, this being echoed in the shape of the window frame, which was straight rather than radiused as before. A glass rear passenger window which echoed the door glass was introduced, so that the whole of the side of the car was glazed, allowing the pillarless effect to be retained.

Support for the roof was provided by steel fabrications which met the existing Superleggera structure at the rear quarter pillars. A top-hinged tailgate, in alloy, was provided, as were rather large rear quarterlights. The whole car was lengthened by the usual 4in and the same bumper was used. The filler caps were now let into the top curvature of the rear wing. Forward of the windscreen, the car was unchanged. From a mechanical standpoint, the cars were unaltered, even spring rates and suspension/steering angles remaining the same.

The interior modifications hinged around the provision of storage and carrying capac-

The interior of the Radford, with its rear folding seat, is beautifully executed.

Corsair Estate? Perhaps that is unfair. These cars, and their later DB6 cousins, did suffer from a lack of strength in the pelvic area. The Superleggera tubes were sacrificed for greater space and the body is not held as rigidly in place as on the saloon cars, despite bracing around the door aperture. A sunroof does not help, either.

ity in the back. The rear seat was redesigned very cleverly, allowing it to flip forward and fold flat, creating a flat rear deck.

These vehicles were hugely expensive, being converted from fully-finished DB5s which were then chopped up. To convert such a vehicle now, should someone wish to do it, would probably cost about the same as a reasonably new Range Rover, the existence of which rather obviates the necessity for an Aston Martin estate car. Actually, these cars were described as shooting brakes, the first one being re-numbered with an 'SB' suffix.

To undertake the reconversion of a Radford car back into saloon form should, on the other hand, be a very straightforward exercise – just imagine that a telegraph pole has been dropped upon it and start from there. Opinion differs as to whether a Radford car is worth more, less, or the same as a saloon. If more, it can hardly be more than the price of a better vehicle. If less, it

can hardly be less than the cost of conversion back to standard. If the same, I should be most surprised. It really rather depends upon whether you are buying or selling. Its curiosity value probably reflects a similar margin to other specialist coachbuilders' efforts on certain other cars, for better or worse. But I should love to see a DB 'Woody'.

The few Radford DB6 models follow a basically similar pattern to the DB5, within the limits of the later model's similarity to its antecedent. They will not be described here, not because a discreet veil should be drawn over them, but because there were only seven of them to start with.

The idea, though, was a sound one, given the times. Probably the main reason that Panelcraft produced only one DBS estate car was that a decent upmarket vehicle existed by then in the form of the Range Rover. Possibly this was a pity, as Panelcraft did a rather nicer job on the DBS, in my view, altering its appearance very little.

Like the short chassis Volante, the Radford estate uses DB6 (Triumph) rear lamps, which make the bumper reflectors unnecessary. Hella number plate lights and a Lucas reverse lamp complete the electrical extras. We are unsure about the origin of the rear screen and locking handles, but the latter seem to be later replacements.

The DB6 and DB6 MkII

The first departure from the original concept, the DB6 is, in fact, more changed than it appears. Despite looking bulkier, its weight is very similar to the DB5, the platform chassis being rather more effectively employed. 'Superleggera' really only pays lip service to the original idea.

Of all the models examined, this is the one, apart from the Rapide, which is the most distinguishable from its stablemates. Although it uses the same basic engine as its predecessors, it is somewhat different under the skin, albeit in small ways. It owes much to the various improvements which took place not only to the mechanical components of the DB4s, but also, from the point of view of body design, to the experience gained in racing. Despite its bulky appearance, it is more aerodynamic and extremely stable at high speed, a speed which is truly sustainable. Of all the cars studied in this book, I regard the DB6 as the most flexible and practical, even if it's not the most attractive.

CHASSIS

Of two main reasons why the DB6 can be considered to be an entirely separate model, despite being derived from the DB4, the first is the chassis. For the first time since DP184, the chassis layout and function was reassessed.

The structure was lengthened to allow greater passenger capacity in the rear, always a complaint about the DB4 and 5 models. The wheelbase was altered for the first time, increasing by 4in to 102in. The front and

rear overhang remains the same, so that overall length also increased by 4in. Inevitably, the glorious proportions of the DB4 are somewhat distorted, the wheelbase increase leaving the bonnet appearing to be shorter, although it isn't. The ratio between those two dimensions is unavoidably spoiled.

Apart from the length, the platform itself is as for the DB5, constructed of the same materials and in the same way. The superstructure, though, is completely different. Due to the increased length of chassis and body, and the fact that this occurred towards the rear of the car, the decision was taken to support the rear bodywork with the same structures as used at the front of the previous models – folded sheet metal frames, rather than the steel tubing previously employed at the rear. This departed from the Superleggera design in detail rather than spirit, and produced another benefit. The bodywork could be more fully attached to the frame, so less metal could be used. The whole car is a mere 17lb heavier than the DB5, despite the standardisation of several previously optional items.

The chassis itself is more or less the same weight, despite its extra length. It has always been a commonly held view that the DB6 is

The 'Kamm' tail and rear threequarter treatment hint at both the Zagato DB4GT and the project cars. It grows on you.

DB6 wheels are invariably chromed.

a much heavier car than the DB5 – it is not. It is much heavier than the early DB4, but the biggest weight gain in the whole series came with the DB4/DB5 transitional models. Clearly, the modifications made to the DB6 chassis are comparatively minor, but the practical benefits are disproportionately large. Greater body rigidity is achieved, the rear threequarter panels acting in a more load bearing capacity, and the DB6 can carry four adults in reasonable comfort.

FRONT SUSPENSION

Fairly predictably, there is nothing new here. The entire layout from the DB5 is retained, except that the castor angle changes to 2¹/₂ degrees if power steering is fitted. Spring rates and damper specifications are unchanged from the DB4 and 5.

REAR SUSPENSION

While the layout remains the same in this department, there is a change in the rear springs. Owing to the heavier weight acting on the rear suspension, the rear springs are slightly less compliant. Constructed of marginally thicker wire, their deflection rate in increased to 142lb in from 132.

Possibly this was not enough, for the DB6 MkII also employed an AEON 520/55 rubber spring in place of a rubber bump stop. This acts on a plate welded to the coil spring carrier on the axle casing. It's a small

point, but the MkII axle cannot be fitted to any other car in the series as a result of this change. Arguably, the rear coils should have been stiffer in the first place. On all DB6s they are now damped by Armstrong 'Selectaride' units as standard.

STEERING

This topic is a little more complex, for three types of steering, two with power assistance, are found on DB6s. The first is straightforward: the unassisted rack and pinion system as used on previous models without modification. The second type is a ZF unit modified by Aston Martin and using a Holbourn-Eaton pump (number 5503). The third is an Adwest unit bought in for the purpose and unmodified. Either type of power steering can be used with either type of optional air conditioning providing the correct drive belts are used. The Adwest system was generally an option on the MkII. Apart from the castor angle already mentioned, the steering geometry is unchanged.

BRAKES

Like the suspension, everything here is as found on the DB5, with the small exception that at chassis 4045 (saloon) and 3736 (Volante) the servo units become Girling type 2B instead of 2A. Calipers, discs and swept area (at 468 sq in) are unchanged. The vacuum reservoir is also present on the Vantage model, as with the DB5.

The DB6 MkII has wider (6in rim) wheels, à la DBS, with lipped arches to accommodate them.

REAR AXLE

There is no longer a choice of final drive ratios for the manual car, merely one default ratio which is new, of 3.73:1. This gives a top gear ratio of 3.11:1 and 25.62mph per 1000rpm, allowing a theoretical maximum speed of 154mph.

The automatic car uses a default ratio of 3.54:1, the same as the standard axle on the DB4, but a 3.73:1 unit was optional. No-one need be in any doubt that an automatic DB6 with this optional axle is something of a lemon; an optimistic top speed of something like 125mph can be calculated, assuming the torque converter is working, and provided that the power loss generated by this appliance can be made up by obtaining a good run-up to maximum rpm.

The axle, of course, is again the familiar Salisbury 4HA unit, the casings being the same for either of the ratios offered – excepting the unique nature of the MkII already mentioned. Strangely, there does not seem to have been a 3.54:1 axle offered for the manual car. Again, a Powr-Lok limited-slip diff is an option.

WHEELS & TYRES

These were as for the DB5, with the exception that the DB6 MkII used the wheels designated for the concurrent DBS model – hence its widened wheelarches. These were 15in wheels with a 6in rim which wore 8.15 x 15 crossply tyres. All wheels are chromed.

ENGINE

There were some interesting developments here, many of which have been exploited by modifiers of earlier cars. The basic engine offered was exactly the same as for the DB5 saloon, delivering 282bhp. The Vantage engine, the number still suffixed by a 'V', had an increased compression ratio of 9.4:1 to give 325bhp at 5750rpm, but used the same cams and valves as before.

There were, however, three further stages of tune which are identifiable within the Vantage designation. The first, 'VA', entailed the use of an inlet cam to the same profile as the DB4GT exhaust cam. It is not the same cam, of course, as it merely uses the same lobe size proportional to the shaft diameter, the GT camshaft being thinner. On this engine, the inlet valve now opens at 38 degrees BTDC and closes at 70 degrees ABDC, while the exhaust valve opens at 66 degrees BBDC and closes at 26 degrees ATDC. Valve springs are unchanged. In addition to this, the Weber carburettors are rejetted.

The other stages of tune, designated 'VB' and 'VC', are really a function of further rejetting of the carburettors. Thus, an engine which is suffixed 'VA' or 'VB' can be made to 'VC' specification by working on the carburettor jets. Details are given in the fuel system section. All Weber MkII Vantage engines are jetted to 'VC' specification.

If an engine is found to be suffixed 'S', it

has been lifted from a DBS model and is not original to a DB6 – but it is the same engine. Stroboscopic timing for all stages of tune is close at around 30 degrees.

The DB6 engine is the final manifestation of the six-cylinder Marek design. The 4-litre unit was used from the introduction of the DB5 until the end of July 1973, its last application being in the AM Vantage model. Thus, in 4-litre standard form, it enjoyed a production life of 10 years almost to the day, and nearly 15 years if its original form is included. Despite its drawbacks, mainly in the area of cooling, it must be counted as one of the 'greats' of post-war engine design.

The matter of power outputs has been a subject of some debate in the years since these cars were new. Many of the claims made by manufacturers in the 1960s have subsequently emerged as somewhat exaggerated. Everyone was at it, from the Italian GT manufacturers to the American muscle car makers.

The hype can be compounded, also, by loose interpretation of the differences between DIN and SAE ratings. For example, the 263bhp quoted by *Road & Track* magazine in April 1962 for a standard DB4 is obviously an SAE figure, possibly extrapolated from the 240bhp (DIN) quoted by Aston Martin itself. If it transpired that the factory's 240bhp was in fact an SAE figure already, then it would seem likely that a truer power output would have been around 220bhp (DIN). Likewise, two tests

The DB6 Vantage engine with its three Weber carburettors. The red reservoir tops are, we suspect, not original.

The exhaust side of the Vantage engine. The manifolding should be silver, and the washer bottle is incorrect.

carried out in 1966 by two American magazines, *Sports Car Graphic* and *Road & Track*, on the same model of DB6 Vantage both quote 325bhp – the former quotes DIN, the latter SAE. From research I have undertaken, it would seem likely that the true DIN output of the 4-litre Vantage engine is something under 300bhp. It must be said, though, that the engineering reports circulated at the works for the first Marek engine in race trim quoted around 280bhp (DIN) in single plug form. Little reason to exaggerate there, I think.

The debate will go on, of course, but the view that a generous interpretation was put upon output at the time seems reasonable enough.

COOLING SYSTEM

The frequent use of air conditioning in DB6 cars affected the cooling system little, except to disrupt airflow through the already less than generous radiator core. This necessitated the use of a 10lb pressure cap as opposed to the previous 7lb one; the water pump seal was upgraded correspondingly to 14lb. Aside from that, the system soldiers on as before.

EXHAUST SYSTEM

This is like the DB5's but correspondingly longer. The extra 4in is in the centre pipe between the silencers, which are the same.

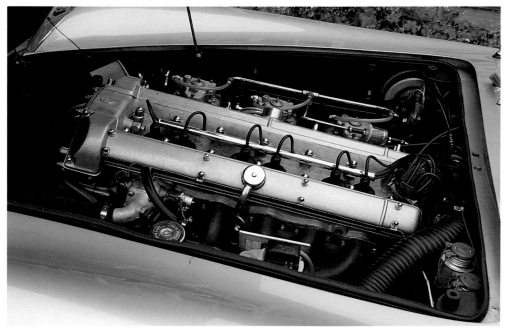

CARBURETTORS & FUEL SYSTEM

The standard DB6 engine used the same triple SU HD8 carburettors as the DB5, with UX needles specified. The 'V' Vantage engine used the same 45DCOE9 Weber carburettors as the DB5 Vantage, jetted as before, with the exception of the idling jet, now a 50F6 type. The 'VA' Vantage engine uses a 140 main jet, 90 air correction jet, a 45 accelerator pump jet, a 45F10 idling jet and a 200 needle valve. The 'VB' Vantage engine uses a 145 main jet, a 125 air correction jet, the same accelerator pump jet, a 50F10 idling jet and the same needle valve. The 'VC' Vantage uses the same specification except that it reverts to the 50F6 idling jet and uses a 250 needle valve. Once again, these settings are for the 1960s when 101 octane fuel was plentiful, and, like the ignition timing, they are for information only.

The SU AUF402 fuel pump remains, in the same location, and the fuel strainer and

A standard engine from a DB6. It is externally the same as the other 4-litre motors, from the DB5 onwards.

air filter are as before. The tank is now 19 gallons, placed as before under the rear parcel shelf. Twin filler flaps are still used, but the fillers have their own quick-release covers under the flaps, rather than the combined flap and cap arrangement used before.

An option of AE Brico fuel injection was also offered on the DB6 MkII, which used the same camshafts and valves as the 'VA', 'VB' and 'VC' engines. Both engine and chassis numbers were given an 'FI' suffix, although many of the 46 cars so equipped have been converted subsequently to Weber carburettors. The system was considered to be somewhat fickle, providing sometimes lumpy tickover and unpredictable flat spots.

TRANSMISSION

Like the rear axle, things are, on the face of it, simpler on the transmission side. The DB6 has either a ZF five-speed, manual box (identical to the DB5 type) or the Borg Warner Model 8 automatic. However, three

types of clutch may be fitted to the ZF, each of a different diameter. On cars with Vantage engines, the Laycock unit used on the DB5 is fitted, up to chassis 2989 (saloon) and 3600 (Volante); for standard cars, chassis 3167 (saloon) and 3651 (Volante) are the relevant cut-off numbers. Subsequent to those numbers, irrespective of tune, a Borg & Beck 9½in single-plate diaphragm is used up to engine number 4159, after which a 10½in unit made by the same firm is substituted.

Plenty of scope there for confusion, I think, particularly when the happy restorer discovers that the Laycock clutch employs a different bellhousing from that used on the Borg & Beck units, and that even the Laycock bellhousing changes at engine 2488. By way of consolation, though, the master and slave cylinders are the same, whatever clutch is used.

The Borg Warner Model 8 uses a torque converter and three-speed gearbox, which delivers a highest ratio of 1:1 and a lowest of 4.8:1 into the differential. Thus, at the

wheels, the range is 3.54:1 to 16.99:1, these ratios in forward gears using the standard final drive. Similarly, the alternative axle delivers 3.73:1 down to 17.9:1. The change points within the gearbox offer sufficient overlap to confuse the device at low and intermediate speeds, up to about 40mph. After that, it lollops along, gobbling engine power and leaving the driver in some doubt as to who is really in control. Not surprisingly, a cottage industry has grown up converting cars back to manual specification, so at least Borg Warner spares are in plentiful supply.

ELECTRICAL EQUIPMENT & LAMPS

There are few changes to the DB5 set-up in this department. All major components are the same, although the distributor is now a Lucas 25D6-41083, with a 423153 contact set. There are three fuse boxes rather than four,

The new air intake. On some cars it has to cater for an oil cooler, an automatic transmission radiator and an air-conditioning panel.

The DB6 tail badge, and the tail lamp unit also fitted to the Triumph TR4A and 5.

one each of Lucas types 543, 828 and 62. The number plate light is now different, the Hella/Volkswagen unit being supplanted by a Lucas 550. The reversing lamp, a Lucas 661, moves from the rear light cluster to between the two rear quarter-bumpers. Although the headlamps remain Lucas F700, the side lamps and front flasher are separated again, like the DB4; they are Lucas 594 and 658 respectively, the former now being amber. The tail lamp cluster is now Lucas 669, as used on Triumph TR4A and 5 models.

BODY & BODY TRIM

The bodywork of the DB6 is the other feature which sets it apart from its predecessors. It is still made of 16swg alloy, but, as mentioned, the method of attachment to the frame now uses entirely the techniques employed at the front of previous cars, there no longer being any Superleggera-style tubing.

The roof and rear pillars of the car are now shaped by steel fabrications, the alloy being clenched around them, giving the outer skin much greater contact with its supports and feeding more of the loads actually into the body. In short, the body is now rather more structural. Given that less steel is used this way, much of the weight increase in the chassis is offset by savings in the superstructure.

There are also important styling changes. The Kamm tail, first used on the DP212,

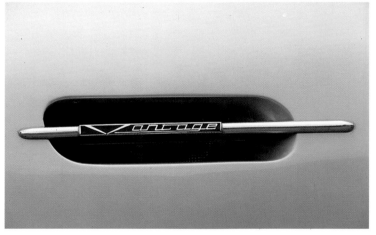

The 'Vantage' legend on the side air vent.

DB6 side badge.

The DB6 has two door ashtrays and the V pattern of stitching on the seats replaces the fluted type of the DB4/5.

214 and 215 project competition cars, was introduced in order to reduce drag, which drops to a coefficient of .36. Wheelbase apart, the DB6 body shares very similar proportions with the DB4GT Zagato, and the rear quarterlights are clearly derived from the shape used on those cars. Front quarterlights are used, too, for the first time since the DB2 series, convertibles aside. The windscreen angle is less raked, in order to raise the roofline, which now converges with the rear deck at the extreme visual rear of the car. The lines are blended together in a tail spoiler, the centre of which is created by a retrousse bootlid. This obviously has the effect of exerting modest rear downforce, which transforms the high speed handling characteristics of the car. The overall effect of the body changes is to increase rear legroom and headroom by around 1in each, but boot space is reduced, in part due to the smaller bootlid that is dictated by the presence of a larger rear window. All this adds up to only modest achievement for such a redesigned body.

At the front, the old aperture for the oil cooler is enlarged. After all, under some circumstances, it has also to provide for cooling air for the automatic transmission oil cooler as well as the condenser for the air conditioning! The enlarged space is fitted with a grille of three horizontal bars, crossed by three vertical ones, the latter lining up with the vertical bars of the radiator grille.

New quarter bumpers without overriders are used, front and rear, and the badging

Quarterlights were now used on a saloon for the first time since the DB2 series. Owners have found that the method of closing can be less than satisfactory, sometimes giving rise to excessive wind noise.

style of the DB5 is retained. A Vantage model is identified by a badge to that effect on the trim of the wing vents on either side, replacing the plain aluminium item used on the standard car (DB5 models also used this feature). The Superleggera badges are retained until 1967, at about chassis 3000, after which they are deleted, due to the unfortunate demise of the Touring company. The DB6 MkII model has the same appearance, save for the addition of flared wheelarches to accommodate wider wheels.

The DB6 Volante

This is the only David Brown Volante. The rest are convertibles, dropheads, whatever, but not Volantes. In AMOC circles, at least, there is no punishment too severe for this solecism. It means 'Flyer', despite the fact that the DB6 Volante is almost the heaviest of the lot.

Perhaps the Kamm tail does not sit as happily on an open car as on a saloon?

Cockpit of the DB6 Volante in this case a MkII.

The roofline is a little higher, the cabin a little longer. There was no hardtop offered, although at least one was made to special order.

This device is the motor for powering the hood mechanism. When this motor is fitted, under the right-hand rear seat, the battery moves back to the boot.

Numbering has started to become rather more complicated. Squinting down past an SU carburettor, we can see that this is DB6Mk2VC (Volante Convertible) 3782 R with engine number 4693. The anomaly between engine and chassis number (they were usually close) is explained by the fact that the model was produced in parallel with the DBS (not DBS6) which started using batches from the DB6 sequence as early as 1967. If a 4-litre engine is suffixed 'S' then it means that it is from a DBS. It is a good idea to check this on DB6 models, even if the engine and chassis numbers are comfortingly close.

Having dealt with the short chassis Volante under the DB5, we can now come to the true DB6, built on a DB6 chassis with a DB6 chassis number. Of course, there are two designations, Volante and MkII Volante, but they are to all intents and purposes the same apart from the few differences already mentioned.

In common with the now established practice at Newport Pagnell, the basic DB6 platform was modified to compensate for the lack of a roof. The work done was similar to that performed on the DB4 and 5: mainly strengthening around the sill area, aft of the B-post and across the pelvis of the car. Due to the extra length of the car, problems are still encountered at the rear deck, but evidence suggests that this convertible is the strongest of all. Certainly, the scales would confirm this, as the car is heavier than the saloon, making it the heaviest car in the DB4, 5 and 6 range. Arguably, it is not as elegant as the previous models, as the Kamm tail does not sit as well on an open car as it does on a saloon, but that is a question of opinion.

Basically, the Volante is to the DB6 what the other convertibles are to their saloon counterparts. Like them, the car has quarterlights but no windowframes. No hardtop was offered, perhaps because the car was heavy enough already! Body fittings and interiors are as for the relevant saloon model, as are engine and transmission options. The hood is power operated by a combination of hydraulic rams and electric motor from chassis 3600.

Buying Guide

This is an area which has been, is and always will be a difficult subject. It brings you into contact with human nature at close quarters – yours and other people's! The most important thing to decide is your choice of model, provided that reading this book has not put you off entirely.

The most numerous model today is probably the DB6, for several reasons. First, more of them were made – some 1570 saloons, 245 of which are MkIIs. Second, they are newer. Third, hardly any of them have been turned into racing cars. The DB5 saloon, of which 898 examples were made, will probably come next despite the fact that fewer DB5s were made than DB4s. The earlier model production included 1040 saloons, but the attrition rate is high on the DB4s and they are also the favourites for club racing, being the lightest of all.

So far as the varying characteristics of each model are concerned, basically the younger the car, the more comfortable it is, although arguably a tired DB6 is no more civilized than a tired DB4. The 6 is probably a nicer touring car, the 4 more agile. The 5 has characteristics of both, but is more like the 4 to drive, being so similar in concept. There is no reason to avoid an automatic car, provided you get the chance to compare it with a manual one, but the performace and petrol consumption are generally inferior – which is the price you pay for leisurely motoring. All models are quite practical to use regularly, provided precautions are taken to engineer out a few of the somewhat anachronistic features which characterise them, particularly cooling and cabin comfort.

Let us assume that your mind is made up, though, and you proceed to see a sample of what is available: ". . . 1961 DB4 Vantage, very good engine, nice interior, much money spent, needs detailing. Rare model, interesting history, etc . . ."

Right, what exactly is it? The best case is that it is a good honest Series Two, Three or Four, with a file of bills representing sensible expenditure, including chassis work. Unfortunately, it cannot be an original Vantage, because the Special Series engine was not fitted until 1962 at chassis 839 of Series Four. It may have been properly upgraded to Special Series level, or it may not. Nonetheless, it could still be a nice car, incorrectly described.

On the other hand, it could be a Series Two, Three or Four with an original, mouldy, smelly interior, rotten sills, an engine which wouldn't pull your socks up despite the fact that a used cylinder head from a crashed DBS has been plonked onto the block, and a rear axle no longer properly connected to the chassis. It may have enjoyed a wipe over with two-pack despite the fact that filler has been substituted for hard work in all the important places. Few of the instruments will work, the electrics are a confection of unattributable spaghetti and it will overheat. It was possibly owned once by Peter Sellers, but, "we are waiting for the service history, and of course, it will be fully serviced and MoT'd prior to delivery (in our workshop which resembles the inside of a wet coal mine)."

The point is, that, from a distance, either case might seem to apply. Research shows that, like interviews, the decision is made by a buyer within minutes of seeing a car. It is, after all, an Aston Martin, and on the face of it, seems good value. Lesson one: good value is seldom an absolute. Typically, poor cars are priced at a level which seems attractive, but seldom is over time. Buy in haste, repent at leisure.

When surveying a particular car, look at it, all around, from a distance of around 15ft, outdoors on a clear day, not in an ill-lit showroom. Look from an oblique angle at ground level. Are there any ripples, dents or areas of flatness in the paint? Check consistency of shut lines. Are there any high spots or low spots? Is it standing squarely? Approach it. Inspect the paint closely, especially those areas where alloy is supported by steel. Feel under the wheelarches and along the bottom of the doors. In the first case, you are looking for filler, in the second, holes.

Smell the interior and look under the carpets. Push the brake pedal hard, not to test the brakes, that comes later, but to make your first check on the pedal box. Lift the ribbed rubber sill covering and poke about with a thin screwdriver. If the sills are internally rotten this may give you a hint, at the edges of the floor. Are the seats worn or cracked?

Now for the engine. Check the oil. Is it clean and at the right level? Are the hoses and gaskets recent? Is it warm? Why? It is better to start a car from cold. If the bores are worn, this will tell you. Either way, look at the oil pressure. It should jump smartly to the required level and stay there. You should just be able to hear the valvegear, as a light gnashing noise with no individual ticks discernible. When thoroughly warmed, raise the revs sharply and lift off. Is there any thrash in the timing chain? Is there any blue smoke coming out of the exhaust? Is the oil pressure steady or fluctuating with the revs? It should go up quickly and down slowly. Switch off.

Put the car on a lift, having first jacked up all four corners to check the solidity of the jacking points. Go underneath. Now that the car is hot, watch for oil leaks and coolant leaks. If you can leave the motor running, so much the better. Check the chassis, starting at the back with the radius arm mounting points. Probe the boot floor, the sills (for filler), the jacking points and the pedal box. At the front, inspect the chassis where the lower wishbone connects. Is there evidence of regular greasing?

Now, let the car down and take it for a drive. It is hot, so you can set off briskly, having established that the tyres are legal and that the brakes do not pull to one side or the other. Trundle along in second, and lift off. You are listening for clunks at the back. Brake gently. You are listening for clunks at the front. Staying in second, accelerate smoothly, watching the oil pressure. It should still be steady, but possibly a little more responsive than before. Check the mirror for blue or black smoke – engines behave very differently when under load. Return whence you came, sit down and check through the service history and bills.

A word about service histories and bills. It is not unknown for a photocopied pile of bills to be attributed to more than one car. This happened to a friend of mine when he bought a DB2. After the oil and water were blended nicely to the consistency of chicken gravy, he called the specialist whose bills he thought he had. It transpired that the rebuild invoice, amongst the large pile of bills acquired with the car, was for an entirely different vehicle, also part of the same vendor's stock. My friend's engine seemed to have been cobbled together by an incompetent blacksmith.

Obviously, there are many more situations which are more straightforward and pleasurable. Dealing with a specialist who has the facilities, the attitude and a track record of straight dealing is always worth extra cost. Good news travels quickly, so ask around.

Back to our DB4. If you are satisfied that you are on the right track, have the vehicle checked out by a specialist, or a motoring organisation. You should have made copious notes. Give them to the inspecting expert. They will help him. You may assume that a car which needs work will be priced so that you, the buyer, will have to spend more money to put it in good condition than a good one will cost. Always remember that it will cost the same to get the work done whatever the car is worth.

In short, if it really is a good car, think about buying it. If it is indifferent, think hard. A car should have at least one good feature about it, hopefully structural. If you have to choose between a good chassis and a ruined engine, or a ruined chassis and a good engine, choose the former, bearing in mind that chassis work which you then have to do will also ensure that paintwork is needed. Astons seldom 'just need paint'.

Frankly, the interior and engine bay are the last things you should worry about. My experience, for what it's worth, is that buying a very good car or a wreck have equal merits. Buying a tired but running example is fine, but if you cannot buy it at the right price, lie down in a darkened room until the thought passes. All this may appear hard on certain elements within the motor trade, but, I can assure you, I am no harder on them than they have been on me.

Of course, cars can be bought in other ways. Privately, for example. Many 'private' sales are, in fact, dealers attempting either to get around Capital Gains Tax or dispose of cars which they have just bought, or cannot sell at auction, by putting them out through other people. A genuine private sale should allow you access to all documentation, including registration. "Waiting for the log book and service history" (see above) is an obfuscation which can slide off the tongue of such people with the same ease as a sea lion off a wet rock. If the person has not owned the car very long, then polite queries as to the nature of the "genuine reason for sale" might legitimately be posed. Proposed emigration is the usual, which rather begs the question of why the car was only acquired last week.

Auctions are great fun. Not only do you get the rare opportunity of rubbing shoulders with "genuine reasons for sale" about to happen, but you also get to make very fast decisions indeed, having as you do to compete both in order to inspect and buy the car. I have a policy for auctions which has stood me in very good stead over time. Attend the auction and obey all the sensible rules of setting a price limit and so forth, then, assuming you still have nothing, go back afterwards and look through the unsold lots. Unknown quantities are what you are looking for, like cars that run badly or will not start. You can also observe what has dripped out of them overnight. The auction process is not as amusing as the viewing, but I recommend it if only for the sake of interest. Over time, you will make friends with all those vehicles whose sole purpose in life seems to be to accompany their doting owners from venue to venue.

Ultimately, the only enjoyable way to buy an Aston Martin is from someone who knows his or her car. Sit down, over refreshment, read the service history, ask the questions, inspect and drive the car, trust your judgement, repair to the local hostelry and haggle in a friendly manner. There should be nothing at all artificial about the actual process of two grown-ups doing business, unless someone is being economical with the truth. As it is with private sales, so it is with decent dealers.

Appendix

COLOUR SCHEMES

All these cars were originally finished in ICI cellulose lacquer, either 'Hilux' or 'Metallichrome' finish. The choice of colours available was huge, as the list below testifies. So far as combinations of trim and paint are concerned good taste was the main influence at work here, at least as far as the manufacturer was concerned. Any doubts as to the original colours and combinations can be checked with the works build sheet, or the build sheet from another car if a change of paint and/or trim is desired.

DB4

GREENS

Sea Green	ICI 3636
Brunswick Green	ICI 3176
British Racing Green	ICI 4460
California Sage	ICI 2629
Goodwood Green	ICI 3438
Moss Green	ICI 2073
Aqua Verda	ICI 3414

BLUES

Blue	ICI XX90
Oxford Blue	ICI 113
Cerulian Blue	ICI 7662
Ice Blue	ICI 2301
Delphinium Blue	ICI ?
Elusive Blue	ICI 2553
Midnight Blue	ICI 2039
Pacific Blue	ICI 3297
Wedgwood Blue	ICI 3145
Blue Sierra	ICI 2803
Imperial Blue	ICI 5531
Ming Blue	ICI 4433
Dark Blue	ICI 5541
Mineral Blue	ICI ?
Caribbean Pearl	ICI 2627
Turquoise	ICI 5193
Aegean Blue	ICI 4391
Mountain Blue	ICI ?
Azzuro Blue	ICI 3170
Sapphire Blue	ICI ?

GREYS

Moonbeam Grey	ICI ?
Shell Grey	ICI 2128
Tudor Grey	ICI 2023
Snow Shadow Grey	ICI 2317
Black Pearl	ICI 2628
Pearl Grey	ICI 2494
Platinum Grey	ICI 3659
Cumberland Grey	ICI ?
Silver Grey	ICI 3314
Silver Birch	ICI 2829

REDS

Garnet	ICI 6316
Regal Red	ICI 2642
Peony Red	ICI 8450
Rosso Rubino	ICI 3194
Cardinal Red	ICI 5776
Carmine Red	ICI 8616
Dubonnet Rosso	ICI 2642
Fiesta Red	ICI 6192
Fire Engine Red	ICI ?
Bright Red	ICI 3692
Roman Purple	ICI 6193

WHITES, YELLOWS, CREAMS, ETC

Broken White	ICI DA88
Desert White	ICI 3267
Old English White	ICI 2680
Porcelain White	ICI 3776
Ivory White	ICI 2379
Pale Primrose	ICI 3297
Dolphin Bronze	ICI 2556
Rose Beige	ICI 2042
Sand	ICI 2559

There were, of course, many other colours from which an owner could choose. Most of the colours above were listed as available for models after the DB4, together with others which were introduced later. Several colours from the above list were also available for the DB MkIII, which was for a while produced alongside the DB4 Series One.

Aston's Racing Green is often held to be California Sage, but it would seem that the Aqua Verda listed last is a more likely candidate for that. Technically, it was a DB2 colour, but both 1VEV and 2VEV wore it at one stage or another, as did certain of the DBR cars.

DB5

Most of the DB4 colours, plus the following:

GREENS

Edinburgh Green	ICI ?
Sage Green	ICI ?

BLUES

Dawn Blue	ICI ?
Sierra Blue	ICI ?
Metallic Blue	ICI ?
Bright Blue	ICI ?

GREYS

Light Grey	ICI ?
Mist Grey	ICI ?
Lavender Grey	ICI ?
Highland Granite	ICI ?
Oystershell Grey	ICI ?
Charcoal Grey	ICI ?

WHITES, YELLOWS, CREAMS, ETC

Ermine White	ICI ?
Golden Sand	ICI ?
Amoranto Roma	ICI ?

DB6

Most of the DB4 and DB5 colours, plus the following:

GREENS

Deep Carriage Green	ICI 3716
Tudor Green	ICI 4610
Tudor Green Cosmic Fire	ICI 5545M

BLUES

Cambridge Blue	ICI 5534
Cambridge Blue Cosmic Fire	ICI 5547
Imperial Blue Cosmic Fire	ICI 5543
Midnight Blue	ICI 2039

GREYS

Ascot Grey Cosmic Fire	ICI 5540
Cardinal Grey	ICI 2555
Tankard Grey Cosmic Fire	ICI 5549
Moorhen Grey	ICI 2464

REDS

Brilliant Fast Red	ICI 3692
Dubonnet	ICI 2400
Red Ochre	ICI 2468
Royal Claret Cosmic Fire	ICI 5544
Royal Claret	ICI 4611

WHITES, YELLOWS, CREAMS, ETC

Cornish Gold	ICI 4609
Cornish Gold Cosmic Fire	ICI 5548
Autumn Gold	ICI 2951
Autumn Gold	ICI C394B

Not all these colours are available now with the same combination of name and number, of course, as even the imagination of paint manufacturers has its limits.

The materials used for the upholstery of all these cars were provided by Connolly Bros of London. For all practical purposes, there is no difference between the DB4, 5, 6 and GT in terms of the actual leather which is used. The hide was treated in the manner described earlier, with a nitrocellulose lacquer on a smooth grain, the resulting effect marketed by Connolly as 'Vaumol'. The exact specification will be found on the factory build sheet and is represented by a number group, prefixed 'VM'. The 'L' suffix denotes a 'Luxan' finish which is slightly grained. As a rule, seat upholstery did not use contrasting piping.

The colour choices typically available through the range were as follows:

TRIM COLOURS

Red	VM 3171
Black	VM 8500
Beige	VM 3234L
Tan	VM 846L
Cream (DB4, DB5)	VM 3323L
Green	VM 3124L
RAF Blue	VM 3244
Midnight Blue	VM 3015
Dark Blue	VM 3282
Grey (DB4)	VM 3230
Grey (DB5, DB6)	VM 3393

Obviously, a company like Aston Martin is always in a position to offer special finishes and effects, so no-one need be too surprised if a car turns up with the remains of Zebra skin seats or a brocade headlining. Fortunately, this appears to be a remote possibility from my studies.

Headlinings are generally in the textured vinyl which has been described, although some cars have been seen with West of England cloth. There have been examples spotted with other headlinings, but these are generally cars which have been restored with a view to 'customising' and are not original.

OPTIONS, EXTRAS & ACCESSORIES

In the 1960s, cars were a little more spartan than they are now, at least in terms of what you actually got for your money at the list price. Like most specialised manufacturers, Aston Martin offered a certain number of accessories, most of them sourced from outside suppliers:

Bray Block Heater
Powr-Lok Differential
Heated Rear Window
Electric Window Lifts
Motorola Radio
Electric Aerial
Fog Lamps
Spot Lamps
Badge Bar
Borrani Wires
Chrome Wires
Whitewall Tyres
Exterior Mirrors
Britax Seat Belts
Overdrive
Borg Warner Auto Transmission
Normalair Air Conditioning
Coolaire Air Conditioning
Special Series Engine
Vantage Engine
GT Engine
Oil Cooler
Selectaride Dampers
GT Instrument Binnacle
Choice of Axle Ratios
Webasto Sunroof
Triple Eared Spinners
Fitted Luggage

PRODUCTION CHANGES

These are dealt with in chassis order, suffixed by (V) Vantage, (Vol) Volante or (E) Engine number; (?) means that I know that the change takes place, but I cannot confirm the exact number at which it does so. I apologise for the frequency of the latter. Although part of the reason for this book is to establish a certain standardization, there comes a point at which guesswork must play a part. All errors are mine.

DB4

131
Window lift gearing raised, channel modified

151
Sundym rear window fitted; window frames fitted, curved glass; overriders and heavier bumpers

161
Boot floor mat made of carpet

181
First gear synchromesh cone added

191
Gearbox mainshaft locking screw added

201
Alloy fan cowl fitted; panel and engine harness modified; bonnet scoop grille moved forward

221
Synchromesh springs strengthened

251
Sump enlarged to 17 pints; dipstick lengthened; extensive modifications to engine mounts; dowels on flywheel housing lengthened; single dowel replaces two on timing cover; water pump fixing stud lengthened; top front oilway on block enlarged; locating dowel added for timing cover; big end nuts no longer castellated; oil pressure relief valve spring strengthened; camshaft covers replaced; camshaft bearing clearances revised; timing case replaced; oil pump output increased; vacuum advance fitted; rear dynamo mounting bracket modified; upper wishbone location to kingpin modified; front discs enlarged from 11½in to 12⅛in; front VB1075 caliper replaces Dunlop VB1033; front pads VB05089 replaced by VB05084; check valve to servo pipe modified; servo mounting clamp modified; vacuum hose from manifold reinforced; check valve ¼in nut changes, Avlok to Nylok; disc shields enlarged; front caliper

bridge pipes modified; rear VB1103 caliper replaces Dunlop VB1046; rear caliper bridge pipes modified; circlips deleted from pedal pivot shaft; master cylinder bracket bolts rearranged; pedal push rods modified; radiator blind fitted; Windtone horn Lucas 69087/90 replaces 69046/7; bulkhead grommets modified; heater front case assembly modifed; bonnet rehung with front hinges; flat window glass introduced; window frames changed to flat; flat rear quarterlight introduced; alloy retainer for quarterlight seal improved; doorlock remote rods strengthened; door glass cant rail seals deleted; door waist rail weatherstrip improved; door pillar seal strip replaced by extrusion; gearing on window winder raised; oil cooler becomes optional; overdrive becomes optional; electric window lifts offered; wiper arms Lucas 54711537 replace 54710006; rear ashtrays fitted

267 (E)
Crankcase breather fitted on nearside engine mount

390
Crank pulley modified; dynamo pulley modified

550
Oil strainer modified

570 (E)
Sump now 21 pints

601
Camshaft breathers modified; electric rev counter fitted; five demister vents fitted; indicator/headlamp flasher combined in one; choke cable clamps modified; twin bonnet supports introduced; handbrake pads detachable from backplates; oil strainer modified again; distributor advance curve modified; coil changed, now HA12 45054; Lucas 2ST solenoid replaces ST950; Lucas 6RA horn and headlamp relay replaces SB40-1; close ratio box introduced; 4.09:1 axle offered as export overdrive option; frame and rear engine mount modified for overdrive; courtesy lights fitted; layshaft rollers modified; front VB1188 caliper replaces VB1075; rear VB1179 caliper replaces VB1103; rear lamp cluster changed to three lenses; protective cover around pedal box fitted; GT engine option listed

696
First gear bearing bush revised

701 (E)
Crankcase breather moved to timing cover

759
Second speed synchro cone modified

766
Air scoop lowered and grille deleted; radiator grille changed to barred type; starter ring and flywheel modified; GT twin-plate clutch introduced; flywheel housing changed; ignition coil now Lucas BA7; ballast resistor Lucas 2BR fitted; ashtray moved from dash to gearbox cover; rear light cluster revised; rear bumper fitted with reflectors; Lucas number plate lamp replaced by Hella; 3.31:1 axle standardised for non-overdrive cars; oil cooler standardised ('delete option'); separate intake fitted for cooler; Special Series engine offered

839
Special Series engine first fitted

943
Wide ratio gears reintroduced; Armstrong 'Selectaride' dampers offered

951
Cowled headlights offered on Special Series; DB4 Vantage announced as separate model; ammeter moved to top centre of binnacle; Lucas 22531A C45 dynamo replaces 22496D; GT instrument panel offered

1001
Body lengthened to 15ft; roofline raised; 15in x 5.5in wheels fitted; Special Series engine now norm; cold airbox fitted; electric fan fitted in front of radiator; automatic transmission offered; front VB1198 caliper replaces VB1188; front VB05290 pad replaces VB05201; rear VB1332 caliper replaces VB1179; distributor advance curve modified; Lucas 47SA ignition switch replaces S60; GT instrument panel now standard; most cars have cowled lamps; ammeter now Lucas CZU26; fuse boxes now Lucas 5FJ

1066
Overdrive 'box now wide ratio as standard

1175
Rev counter drive unit modified

1176(?)
Twin filler flaps offered as option

DB5

1340
ZF five-speed gearbox standardised

1526
Engine-driven fan replaces electric fan

1609
DB5 badges fitted on boot and wings; compression ratio raised from 8.3:1 to 8.9:1; jet needles UX replace UU; Lucas DMBZ6 40981 distributor replaces 40938; Lucas 4TR alternator control replaces 3TR; Lucas 3AW charge indicator replaces 2AW

1609 (?)
Headlamp cowls now chrome-plated

1845 (E)
Main bearing cap torque changed to 60lb (90)

DB6

2442
Window weatherstrip replaced by extrusion

2990 (V)
Borg & Beck 9½in clutch replaces Laycock 10in

3100 (?)
'Superleggera' badge deleted

3186
Borg & Beck 9½in clutch replaces Laycock 10in (all cars); battery moved to offside rear wing

3361 (?)
Thermostat water return valve modified

3552
Cranked gear lever fitted to RHD cars

3600 (Vol)
Power-operated hood fitted

3601 (Vol)
Borg & Beck 9½in clutch replaces Laycock 10in

4045
Girling servo 11B replaces 11A

4160
Borg & Beck 10½in clutch supersedes 9½in item

Despite its length, this list of modifications and amendments is not comprehensive; apart from the DB4 model, which underwent an almost constant metamorphosis, the changes to the DB5 and DB6 models are actually few. I have included those which will make a material difference to a restoration, so that rather than list every nut and bolt which is replaced when a new type of clutch is tried, for example, I have listed that new clutch as a change in itself and left it at that. To list every other connected modification would absorb another book, and, after all, that is what a parts manual is for.

There were other differences as well, particularly with regard to export models. These are generally in the area of lighting, lens colour and certain safety features such as hub spinners or safety belts. Due to the difficulty of ascertaining what current regulations are, I have not included these in the list, as I should hate to be blamed if rear light lenses for a DB6 no longer had to be red in the Lebanon, for example. A general rule in America, though, is that this is usually the case, amber not being allowed. Reimported cars will often be equipped with foreign specification lamps, so obviously this would need to be checked before a night journey is undertaken – it is surprising what MoT examiners can overlook when studying an Aston Martin!

Finally, in deference to those who insist that every Aston Martin is different, I have to say that, superficially, this is correct. I hope, though, that the use of this book will enable an owner or restorer at least to approximate the correct specification of a car before myriad options were fitted or modifications carried out over the years.